D1707658

TWO DIFFERENT
WORLDS

TWO DIFFERENT WORLDS

Christian Absolutes
and the Relativism
of Social Science

Charles E. Garrison

DELAWARE

Newark: University of Delaware Press
London and Toronto: Associated University Presses

© 1988 by Associated University Presses, Inc.

Associated University Presses
440 Forsgate Drive
Cranbury, NJ 08512

Associated University Presses
25 Sicilian Avenue
London WC1A 2QH, England

Associated University Presses
P.O. Box 488, Port Credit
Mississauga, Ontario
Canada L5G 4M2

The paper used in this publication meets the requirements
of the American National Standard for Permanence of Paper
for Printed Library Materials Z39.48-1984.

Library of Congress Cataloging-in-Publication Data

Garrison, Charles E.
   Two different worlds.

   Bibliography: p.
   Includes index.
   1. Social sciences—Religious aspects—Christianity.
2. Christianity and culture.   3. Cultural relativism.
I. Title.
BR115.S57G37   1988   261.5   87-40119
ISBN 0-87413-330-0 (alk. paper)

PRINTED IN THE UNITED STATES OF AMERICA

Contents

Acknowledgments

The acknowledgment of indebtedness is, for me, the discovery of the truth and common experience expressed in what seem to be clichéd phrases. How can I adequately acknowledge the sources from parents, sisters, teachers, ministers, college professors, colleagues, and friends who in many ways—usually unbeknownst to them—have shaped and influenced my thinking and my work? I am most indebted to them and often reflect upon their contributions as they come to mind.

Limiting the specific acknowledgments only to the most immediate and direct contributions, I am indebted for the critical comments of Professor William Swatos, the editorial comments of Jay DeVane and Ann Prezell, and the varieties of assistance including the editorial help of my wife, Maureen. Additionally, I must acknowledge our daughters, Christy and Julie, who not only contribute in many ways but also provide an important stake for us in the future of our world.

TWO DIFFERENT
WORLDS

Part I
Introduction

1

Setting the Stage

Something there is that doesn't love a wall.
Before I built a wall I'd ask to know
What I was walling in or walling out.
                                    —Robert Frost

It happened on the 24 March 1985 telecast of 60 *Minutes,* but the ideas expressed occur repeatedly. "People will be lost who do not take Jesus as their savior!" was the assertion. The response was pointed; "But how can you know this for sure?" The man who made the assertion believed it to be the absolute truth. The man who responded was unsure that such knowledge is possible for thoughtful, reasonable people. It was only a brief verbal jostle but it revealed two different worlds.

This exchange illustrates an underlying cultural division that splits our society into warring camps. On one side are the Christian "absolutists" who believe that their views reflect biblical truth and those who differ with them are in dangerous error. The concept "absolutist" identifies their belief that "truth" is absolute and not relative to any particular culture or situation. That is, their "truth" is true for every person in every place at every time.

The other side is led by those who have been identified as the "New Class." James Hunter uses this term to refer to the most recent historical variation of social class—"a social group distinguished by its special relationship to the means of production." In this case the New Class "most generally consists of those college and professionally trained people who are occupationally associated with the knowledge industry." Put differently, the New Class comprises those who derive their livelihoods from the creation and manipulation of symbols.[1] They are generally well educated and have accepted the prevailing views of higher education. Their beliefs are rooted in the liberal tradition of a rationalistic and secular humanism. They believe that what is called truth is relative, and they find it difficult to tolerate what they regard as the narrowness of the Christian absolutists. Hunter notes that although some of the occupations

13

in this class are not new, the percentage of people they employ has increased dramatically since World War II.[2]

Attacks by Christian absolutists upon the secular humanism of the New Class have received much attention. So also have the charges made in return that Christian absolutism is narrow-minded, authoritarian, and dangerous. Communication between these opposing views is limited, and when it occurs it usually only reinforces the sense of opposition. Actual collisions are limited because of the social wall separating each side from the other. On each side a perception of truth influences its own segment of society and each considers the opposing side to be dangerous. This wall serves well the purpose of walling—to separate and defend—but in doing this it also reinforces the division. Meanwhile, attacks and counterattacks occur in classrooms, churches, school board meetings, letter-to-the-editor columns, and sometimes in courtrooms.

Caught between these two camps is a large segment of people who cannot give unqualified support to either side. Such people value their Christian possibilities, but they also cannot turn their backs on the collective scholarship of the educators. They are unwilling to reduce Christianity to the stereotypes of ignorance and authoritarianism. Yet, they also cannot accept the notion that the educational establishment is some unusual collection of the devious who are determined to destroy all that is decent and wholesome. Many college students continue to be caught in the conflict between their Christian upbringing and the social scientific views of the college classroom. But many who are older are equally caught between these two worlds.

These are people who want to use the best insights wherever they may originate. They have some experiences of both Christian faith and secular education. I meet such individuals every semester in my classes. I meet them in the community. I am one myself. And this is the reason for this book. Is it really necessary to choose one side or the other?

The major thesis of this book is that both camps force false alternatives that neither Christianity nor social science requires. In bypassing these false alternatives some very helpful insights will become evident. Social science, rather than being a destructive force, will be seen to be contributing to a more vital and engaging Christianity. The image of Christianity, in its attitude toward the world, on the other hand, will be radically altered, even though it can still adhere to its basic belief structure. Rather than being a narrow sectarian religion that justifies its own behavior while pronouncing condemnation of all others, it emerges as able to accept quite easily the many religions of our pluralistic world, neither capitulating in its own values nor demanding domination of others.

The ideas I will explore here are not just personal dilemmas. When they emerge into the public forum, collisions are inevitable. The New Class has had important influence on higher education and the public media. Both of these are considered by absolutists to be biased indoctrinators who hide their ideological objectives behind self-described principles of objectivity and science: absolutists believe this to be destructive to our society. To counter this influence, Christian absolutists have built alternative schools and colleges, established publications, and built or purchased numerous radio and television outlets.

Underlying the other issues is a basic conflict regarding the nature of reality: is truth—that which humans can know—absolute and revealed, or is it relative to its social context? And must Christian knowledge be absolute to be true? The New Class looks askance at the Christians who assert absolutes. Like the interviewer on 60 *Minutes*, they ask, "How can you know for sure?" This underlying issue of knowledge is recognized by both sides as each seeks to justify and defend itself against the verbal attacks of the other.

This book explores the basic disagreement that continues to spawn conflict. The exploration is divided into four parts: the first defines the basic issues; the second part draws mainly upon sociology and, to a lesser extent, upon anthropology to develop the secular humanistic side of the issue as shaped by the social sciences; the third part formulates a Christian understanding based upon an analysis of the biblical text; and the final section discusses the conclusions and the implications for both Christians and secular humanists.

Specifying the Conflict

Before the investigation can proceed, care must be given to specify the conflict and the opposing sides. Christian absolutists feel justified in their antagonism toward the New Class of secular humanists. It is their view that secular humanism destroys the capacity of people for belief in any absolute truth—that people under its sway are unable to say that anything is really true or false, good or bad. They would find this expressed in the 60 *Minutes* exchange that did not debate the minister's assertion but questioned that such a claim could be knowable. Absolutists contend that this questioning destroys the foundation for the beliefs and morality of society. The source of what they see as the "cancer" of secular humanism is found in the study of cultural anthropology and the sociology of knowledge. It is expressed most specifically in the social scientists' theory of cultural relativity. As will be discussed in a later chapter, anything that smacks of relativity is open to concerted attack by the absolutists.

The idea of cultural relativity developed from insights gained in anthropological studies of human behavior that compared diverse cultures. Some background on its development will be helpful. In studying alien cultures there slowly emerged the realization that a simple comparison of a foreign culture to one's own would result in misinterpreting what was being studied. The meanings of one culture were not easily translated into another. It became clear, for example, that a word was not simply a label that was attached to represent a reality. If it had been, then translation from one language to another would have been a matter of changing the labels. Instead, anthropologists discovered that language reflects the way people define the world around them. This definition of reality is pervasive within the language but is not translatable. It must be perceived in its own way. The correct words of a translation must be selected only after the context of meaning has been understood.

Linguists involved in translating the Bible long ago recognized that a literal word-for-word translation could be, for some passages, the worst of translations. Eugene Nida, a well-known biblical linguist, has written that "strictly word-for-word renderings inevitably tend to distort the meaning of the source-language message."[3] Translator Ronald Knox has written that "Words are not coins, dead things whose value can be mathematically computed. You cannot quote an exact English equivalent for a French coin. Words are living things, full of shades of meaning, full of associations; and what is more, they are apt to change their significance from one generation to the next."[4] This is an important clue to the problems of cross-cultural understanding.

An illustration of this characteristic can be found in Eleanor Bowen's novel that portrayed her experiences of living in a polygamous culture.[5] She grew up in America but lived as an adult in a society where polygamy was prevalent. Expecting that women who share a husband would be competitive and jealous with each other, she found to her amazement that they were quite happy with their ways. They, however, believed that monogamous wives must be extremely lonely and that life would be difficult in such an arrangement. They felt sorry for the plight of the monogamous wife. It was quite clear that the translation of terms such as "wife" or "polygamy" from one language to another was not simply a change of labels, but that a number of meanings were associated with each term that reflected what was viewed as the appropriate way to live. These meanings, in turn, were derived from basic assumptions about reality.

Each person—whether monogamous or polygamous—viewed his or her own culture as the standard and compared the alternative to that standard. This attitude, called "ethnocentrism," is the normal response of people to alien cultures. The earliest working anthropologists made the same mistake. Attempting to avoid the errors that resulted from this assumption, anthropologists established the working principle that all traits of a culture must be understood in the context of that culture—not the anthropologists' own culture. That is, the meaning of cultural traits must be relative to the culture in which they exist and not an external standard. This was the fundamental idea of cultural relativity: it was a working principle used to avoid the inherent errors of ethnocentrism.

The use of this principle, however, raised the question of how people "know what they know." All cultures convey to their members a body of knowledge that is considered the truth. But how is "the truth" established? This question often makes people uncomfortable. We all have ideas that we assert to be true without any real evidence or without knowing whether there is evidence. We have ideas that we think are "self-evident." But they probably are not self-evident to others. For example, why do polygamists not recognize the superiority of monogamy? The usual explanation implies that the other people are in some sense intellectually or morally inferior. But anthropologists who studied the so-called primitive peoples were forced by the evidence to conclude that they were usually quite developed both intellectually and morally.

In addition to the anthropological evidence, a new area in sociology emerged; it became known as the sociology of knowledge. It sought answers to the question of how a society develops and disperses what it considers to be knowledge. The theory that emerged in the sociology of knowledge was that a society defines as knowledge the sum of conversations among its people. There are some events in which this process can be recognized easily: Harry Truman, whose presidency was maligned in his day, has since become a quite popular president, praised by Republicans and Democrats alike. No new facts have emerged that account for this increased popularity. It has not occurred for other presidents. In the ongoing conversations that define culture, early "facts" and meanings (in this case, about Truman) have been forgotten, and new ones have replaced them.

This process operates in all facets of knowledge. As people talk with each other in their daily lives, they evolve and affirm definitions of what is true. These conversations reflect the empirical experiences of the people as well as their already existing ideas. As ideas are shared and define for people what is true or false and what is good or bad, they make sense, because, as members of the culture, the people have been part of the conversation. What is believed to be knowledge is thus a consequence of social interaction and a result of the conversations of that interaction. All knowledge and all ethics, according to this view, are perceived as valid within the culture that validates them. This is not due to the availability of some external, objective evidence as is conventionally supposed. It is a consequence of the cultural process, and every culture is subject to it. In exploring the question of "how we know what we know," cultural relativity became more than a method of research. It became an assertion about the nature of culture itself.

Cultural relativism, then, is the recognition that a culture—if it is to be accurately understood—must be interpreted in terms of its own system of thinking. Further, what is defined as knowledge within any culture is a consequence of the social interaction in that culture. Therefore, what a society holds to be knowledge will always be relative to the circumstances of that society. Yet, a warning is in order: the process of cultural development and the empirical evidence for cultural relativity is far more involved than these brief statements suggest. There are other factors that must be considered, but this explanation provides a preliminary definition. Cultural relativity has been the subject of extensive research and theoretical examination, not only in anthropology and the sociology of knowledge, but in other areas such as linguistics and communication theory.[6]

Anthropologists did not accept cultural relativity easily but reluctantly because of the accumulating evidence from their research. While social scientists may disagree about some of its technical details, the general meaning used here is widely accepted. They believe that cultural relativity is based upon empirical evidence and is a well-founded working assumption for research in human behavior.

It is crucial to recognize from the outset that the issue of relativity is about knowledge, not reality. A tree is what it is no matter what ideas people have about it. Whether God exists and what God has done or not done does not depend upon our ideas of God. Social science has never disputed the existence of an ultimate reality that, whatever it is, is what it is. Relativity addresses the issue of our knowledge of reality, not the reality itself.

People of most cultures assume that their own knowledge of facts and ethics is more than just a product of their social interaction. To those within a culture, their own ideas seem so obviously true that they wonder why any right-minded person could think otherwise. But Christians have an additional reason for believing that their facts and ethics are not the product of social conversation. They hold the traditional affirmation of Christianity, that its truths are revealed from God, and are to be propagated to all nations. This truth is a special category of knowledge. Furthermore, they believe that it is only through this message that people can gain salvation. Does not this necessarily mean that the Christian message must be considered by the believer to be absolute truth? Does not cultural relativity thus represent an intolerable attack upon Christianity?

Christian absolutists answer these questions affirmatively. They are convinced that Christian truth is not based upon the social conversations of the people in a culture but on God's revelation. As such it must be true for all situations, in all cultures, at all times. It is therefore appropriate to judge all people by these Christian truths.[7] It is, in other words, absolute rather than relative to any circumstances.

Francis Schaeffer, a frequently cited Christian author, has written that Christians and secular humanists have directly opposing views of reality: "These two world views stand as totals in complete antithesis to each other in content and also in their natural results—including sociological and governmental results."[8] To emphasize the point, he adds: "There is no way to mix these two total world views. They are separate entities that cannot be synthesized."[9] What Shaeffer and others define as the Christian world view includes what is referred to in this book as Christian absolutism. The secularist-humanist world view is defined by Schaeffer as "the idea that the final reality is impersonal matter or energy shaped into its present form by impersonal chance."[10] Though this definition of impersonal matter is asserted by some and assumed by others, it is not a necessary thesis of the New Class. The aspect of secular humanism to be considered here is characterized far more by its rejection of any absolute knowledge than by its assertion of materialistic absolutes.

There is, however, a linkage. To the extent that understanding "how we know" causes us to question "what we know," cultural relativism may be experienced by absolutists as destructive to their beliefs. Cultural relativists are scientifically oriented and may seem to hold to materialism. But the consequence of relativism is more firmly rooted in the experience of comparing cultures. When a person reads reports of different cultures, each of which has its own firm belief in its own religion, it is easy to assume that the knowledge each group has of its religion is "nothing but" a tribal ethnocentrism. Indeed, Christians often make this interpretation of other religions.

A turning point may occur if we ask: If it is true for "them," why not for "us"? If others' idea of truth is relative to their culture, then ours must be also. It is in this way that cultural relativism has led to a questioning of absolute truths, including those of Christianity. But, does this mean that cultural relativism is necessarily the enemy of the Christian and the supporter of the agnostic or atheist? Christian absolutists such as Schaeffer are convinced that this is true. If it is so, the collisions would seem to be unavoidable and the walls isolating the two views to be a strategic necessity. But this has not been investigated. The issue has been bypassed. It is the pursuit of the answer to this question that is the central objective of this book.

The Concepts in Conflict

It has already been noted that Christian absolutists believe that cultural relativity destroys belief in both moral standards and Christian truth. As such, relativism is believed to leave no criteria for judging human behavior. Without such criteria for behavior, it is believed, the moral fiber of society is endangered. Relativism is said to be a "spectre" which "haunts human thought."[11] Historian Paul Johnson contends that the murder of the Jews at Auschwitz was a result of the moral relativism of the Nazis.[12] To absolutists, cultural relativism is quite clearly dangerous and writers regularly attack it. The following is an example:

> When the apostolic witness is reduced to culture-bound accounts of encounters with Jesus, we are left without the Word of God in the world.

> Either there is a "transcultural" common truth which is intelligible to "all the nations," or the Great Commission is impossible of implementation.

> To make cultural relativism an absolute is precisely to destroy objective truth and normative values.[13]

Relativists should not make the mistake of thinking that such assertions as Smith has made are found only among uninformed individuals who have not been exposed to the truths of social science. Philosopher Elton Trueblood wrote in 1948 that cultural relativism had already destroyed the possibility of faith for a generation.[14] David Hubbard of Fuller Theological Seminary has said that the "greatest challenges to evangelical Christianity are coming from the behavioral sciences."[15] And sociologist Peter Berger has written that "sociology raises the vertigo of relativity to its most furious pitch, posing a challenge to theological thought with unprecedented sharpness."[16] Berger's view is that "the physical sciences' challenges to theology have been relatively mild" compared to that of cultural relativity.[17] Christian sociologist David Lyon has added: "Relativism is a creeping, cancerous academic affliction from which social scientists are particularly prone to suffer."[18]

On the other side, relativists are very afraid of absolutism. One of the interpretations of science for the public judged to be among the best was Jacob Bronowski's television series and book, *The Ascent of Man*. In the eleventh episode, Bronowski stood in what had once been the Auschwitz prison camp, near a pond whose bottom was said to be white with the ashes of Jews. He dramatically reached down, scooped up some of the stagnant water, looked into the camera and said, "When people believe that they have absolute knowledge, with no test in reality, this is how they behave. This is what men do when they aspire to the knowledge of gods."[19] Bronowski was as certain that the atrocities of Auschwitz were a result of absolutism as Paul Johnson was that cultural relativity was the cause.

This disagreement over the Nazi murder of Jews illustrates a common problem in considering relativism. People often perceive relativism to be such a specter of destruction that they assume it to be present in all social catastrophies. To Johnson, relativism was responsible not only for the actions of Nazi Germany but for the behavior of the communist governments of Russia and China as well.[20] By the definition of relativism used here—and this usage is prevalent in sociology and anthropology—these governments have been absolutist rather than relativist. Their beliefs have been considered by themselves to be right in every time and place rather than shaped by their own time and social circumstances.

Historian Arthur Schlesinger, Jr. has supported Bronowski's interpretation: "Any person who deludes himself into supposing he has special access to absolute truth, whether as revealed by Mark or Mohammed, Marx or Mao, or any other religious or secular prophet, can go about suppressing dissent and persecuting heresy with clear conscience."[21]

Relativists consider history to be rife with episodes of the damage done by absolutist thinking, and Christian absolutist thinking has furnished many of the examples. The Roman Catholic inquisition is often cited, but it is by no means the only example. Keith Roberts cites evidence that from 1400–1700 A.D. between one-half and one million people (mostly women) were burned as witches by European Protestants and Catholics. Two villages were noted in which only one female was left alive after the burnings in 1585.[22] Such fanaticism is often seen to be a result of being a "true believer"—an idea shaped so well in Eric Hoffer's book by that title that it became a part of the collective wisdom of relativists.

The intellectuals who participated in the publication of the *Humanist Manifesto* in 1933 were explicit in asserting their rejection of absolutism in favor of moral relativism: "We affirm that moral values derive their source from human experience. Ethics is autonomous and situational."[23] They also asserted that "religion must formulate its hopes and plans in the light of the scientific spirit and method."[24] This humanistic-relativistic emphasis in social science was expressed by Alfred McClung Lee, past president of the American Sociological Association: "Humanist sociology . . . is existential and relative, not to be diverted into searches for such will-o'-the-wisps as universals, absolutes, and essences."[25]

If humanist-social scientists decree as a basic assumption that science is the measure of truth, and if sociologists are to declare it a useless diversion to search for possible absolutes, then it is understandable when Christian absolutists believe that relativists are unwilling to consider the possibility that traditional Christianity has legitimate claims to truth. Christian absolutists find it alarming not only that secular humanism is based on cultural relativity but also that it opposes absolutism. As such, it is considered to be not just neutral toward traditional Christianity but in basic opposition to it.

What Christians see as truth and morality is regarded by the relativists as dangerous and destructive. Thus Robert Webber's statement: "The most striking and recurring theme which runs through every point [of secular humanism] is that the church and Christianity are the enemy of the people and progress and that man himself has the capacity to save the world."[26]

The lines of conflict are clearly drawn. The differences between Christian absolutism and the cultural relativity of the New Class are not matters of obscure theoretical debate. They are two different worlds. They are derived from differences in the basic ways people perceive the world, including the knowledge and moral principles necessary for the survival of society. It is not just that the two sides disagree but that each considers the other to be extremely dangerous to the human race. Such a division itself is extremely dangerous and leads us back to an adapted version of Robert Frost's basic question about a wall: What is each side walling in or walling out? Is the wall helpful? Would it be wise to reinforce the wall? What would happen if the wall were to be removed?

Identifying the Opponents

So far I have written about absolutists and relativists as if they are as identifiable in real life as males and females. This is, of course, not so. Both come in many shadings. Nevertheless, in some social groups Christian absolutism is so universally and clearly assumed to be true that it makes sense to speak of such people as a category. Similarly, in other circles, the basic tenets of relativism are also assumed with such unspoken agreement that treatment as a category makes sense. Still, it may be helpful to note more specifically some of the aspects which identify those who hold each view.

There is considerable variety among Christian absolutists, and we should be wary of stereotypes. What the absolutists share is an acceptance of what has already been referred to as "traditional Christianity," that is, the belief that the Bible is the authoritative revelation of events surrounding Jesus, who was the Son of God, and other events in God's workings, and that the Bible itself is the revelation of God's message. This definition of traditional Christianity is used because it represents what Protestant fundamentalists believe to be the major tradition. It ignores the traditions of others such as Roman Catholic, Orthodox, and Coptic Christians. Those here labeled as "traditional Christians" identify themselves as part of a tradition of Christian belief that reaches back to the times portrayed in the New Testament and as conveyers of a pure Christianity. The term "Christian absolutists" is used to refer to traditional Christians who believe that Christian truth is both revealed and absolute.

There are other people who consider themselves to be Christians but who would disavow a connection with this traditional Christianity. They have accepted various scientific viewpoints—including that of social science—and have tried to accommodate their Christian faith to scientific views. They do not accept fundamentalist and evangelical beliefs and consider such views to be damaging to the best interests of the real meaning of the Christian religion. These can be categorized as "non-traditional Christians." They have often in the past been labeled as modernists and more recently have usually been tagged as "liberal Christians."

Indeed, scholarly studies of Christianity by Christians have been dominated by individuals who accepted the cultural relativity of knowledge and norms as a basic assumption of their work. These scholars, consequently, have been denounced for this by absolutists who labeled them unbelievers. The scholars have tended to dismiss the absolutists as simply uneducated, uninformed, and irrelevant. These scholars, in addition to their relativism, rejected beliefs that absolutist Christians considered vital.

But can there be a third category—traditional Christians, in the full sense of the term, who are not absolutists? Consistency, presumably, requires that they be given the unwieldy label of "traditional-but-not-absolutist Christians." This position could accept all of the doctrines of traditional Christianity but would not make absolutist assertions about them. This position could be both traditional and relativistic. This possibility has been ignored by both social scientists and theologians; I will explore it in later chapters.

It may be helpful to note that just as there are Christians who are not absolutists, so also are there absolutists who are not Christians. Muslim fundamentalists and Marxist fundamentalists would be examples of non-Christians who also would be opposed to relativistic interpretations. For our purposes here, we will be considering most directly those people who are both Christian and absolutist. Later on, we will also consider the traditional-but-not-absolutist Christian position.

The New Class has already been defined as composed of educated people who are often occupationally associated with some component of the knowledge industry such as educators, journalists, and authors. These are the people who are part of the general spirit of the educated and intellectually oriented sector of our society. They have accepted cultural relativity because it is a part of the intellectual stock which they have absorbed. A hard core of relativists would be the social scientists of cultural anthropology and the sociology of knowledge. There is also a broad category of social scientists and people in other occupations who apply the conceptual framework of the social sciences. There is a still broader array of people who are influenced by these ideas though they may not be aware of the source of their views. The impact of relativism can be found among the uneducated as well as the educated—both asserting the notion that "who's to say" whether any behavior is right or wrong. While these various types of people may share a general relativistic viewpoint, they also generate a variety of interpretations. The relativistic position that will be discussed here will reflect that of cultural anthropology and the sociology of knowledge.

Reasons for Studying the "Wall"

The difference in interpretations between the Christian absolutists and the cultural relativists, the disdain each so often holds for the other, and the lack of communication between them suggests sufficient reason to study the situation just because it exists. These differences pose interesting questions whether one's basic interest is Christianity, cultural anthropology, or sociology. The questions are academic in the sense that thoughtful people will be challenged by them. But they are not "just academic" because they do affect people in their everyday lives. It is important precisely because these two views reflect a division that is central in our society and is being fought over in schools, libraries, churches, political parties, and other groups where important decisions are being made.

While it is true that conflict can be creative, it is not inevitably so. Though this conflict may have creative aspects, there is also a basic inefficiency in it. The polarization of positions and the consequent need to defend those positions is not likely to provide a constructive forum for determining public policy issues. An adversarial stance by Christians to social science makes it difficult for them to use the insights of these same social sciences in other applications. Yet, the understanding of other cultures and communication across subcultures and cultural boundaries is vital for Christian work. In our pluralistic age the aid of the social sciences can be important for all groups, including the churches.

Similarly, when the social sciences believe that they have a basic mission to defend cultural relativity, that very effort to defend is not helpful. It can create a crusading attitude that tends to forego self-criticism and results in narrowness. The consequent zeal to enlighten the absolutists may endanger the efforts by social scientists to critically examine their own positions.

These comments are not meant to suggest that all efforts in the conflict are misguided and should be discontinued. They do not imply that reconciliation will occur if each side understands the other. It is to suggest an application of the maxim that, in conflict, the search for truth is usually the first casualty. It is to suggest that it is time to reassess the conflict to determine if conflict is necessary. It may be that both sides are accumulating positions that are not helpful.

There are other important considerations. Every year students arrive on college campuses from Christian absolutist backgrounds. On campus they encounter professors who call into question those Christian beliefs that have been so much a part of their lives. Many of these students discard their earlier beliefs and accept what they consider to be the more advanced, up-to-date thinking advocated by their professors. Some, of course, resist. Whether those who accept the views of the faculty should be considered as fallen or enlightened depends upon which side one is on. Similarly, whether those who resist are narrow-minded and purposely ignorant, or steadfast and well-grounded, depends upon one's perspective. Some of these students seek literature or counsel on the issue of science and religion, make some type of accommodation, and continue on their ways. This experience has been very common for several generations of college students. It has become almost a tradition.

Educators have often assumed that this conflict would continue until the general educational level of the society had risen and then it would no longer exist. In fact, sociologists have long expected that a rising tide of scientific secularism would engulf the dwindling number of people who cling to traditional Christian doctrines. The classic sociologist, Emile Durkheim, wrote in 1912 that, "the old gods are growing old or already dead."[27] He predicted that new religions were likely to emerge that would emphasize one's social ties but would be devoid of theism.

Bonhoeffer wrote almost half a century ago that man was then "come of age" and required a "religionless Christianity."[28] By this he meant that people no longer required precisely those things which characterize the Christian absolutes. His "religionless Christianity" roughly approximated a Christianity minus those beliefs and norms upon which the absolutists insist. The point here is that half a century ago, it was thought that it would be necessary for the church to adopt this religionless Christianity if it were to survive.

In the 1960s, writers were still expecting that they were in an era when the church, if it was to continue to find adherents, would have to discard those beliefs and norms on which absolutists insist. Bishop A. T. Robinson of the Church of England published in 1963 his expression of this idea in a much read and discussed book, *Honest to God.* In 1965 social theologian Harvey Cox published his celebration of this new religion in his book, *The Secular City.* And a most important sociology book on religion by Peter Berger, *The Sacred Canopy,* was published in 1967, that set forth a view consistent with these, though with a different tack. Berger also saw society as increasingly secular. The traditional doctrines of Christianity, he believed, could not be sustained in such a society. It was necessary, therefore, for Christians to isolate themselves from society if they were to sustain the plausibility of their beliefs. Berger's book remains valuable for its basic sociological insights. However, his prediction that Christian believers would be a dwindling minority clearly looks inaccurate in the 1980s.

In 1972, five years after Berger's book was published, Dean Kelley published his evidence that the absolutists were the growing segment of Christianity in his book *Why Conservative Churches are Growing.* That same year *Unsecular Man* by Andrew Greeley was published. In it he contended that the population was not secularized as had been supposed but quite able to accept wholeheartedly the tradtional Christian ideas. His conclusion was based on two empirical observations: first, "the available statistical data simply do not indicate a declining religiousness in the United States"; secondly, "the resurgence of bizarre forms of the sacred on the secular university campus has now persisted long enough that it cannot simply be written off as a passing fashion."[29]

The rising force of the Christian absolutists was quite evident in the presidential elections of 1980 and 1984.[30] The impact was not as clear in the 1986 election. Whether it has peaked will not be known until several more elections have occurred. Certainly the media have expressed much interest in the phenomenon over several years. It is likely that, as with all social movements, there will be at some point a peaking and a leveling if not a decline. This fact notwithstanding, the force of the Christian absolutists is clearly not something that was anticipated by the social scientists or commentators.

The Reverend Jerry Falwell has stated that there are four new Christian schools being established every day. At the time of his survey he counted twenty thousand such schools in the United States. He cited that, in addition, there were sixteen hundred Christian radio stations, with a new one being started every week. By his figures, sixty-five Christian television stations existed, with a new one going on the air every month.[31] Even if one believes these statistics to be exaggerated, no one can deny that the expansion of Christian absolutist activities has been unexpected and is a matter of considerable consequence.

These programs could not expand without widespread support. Across America there is obvious enthusiasm for the expansion of Christian absolutism. The desire for a religionless Christianity is associated now with churches that are dying. It seems clear that the ability to sustain traditional Christian beliefs is not currently in jeopardy. This means that projections for the future based upon current data must indicate that there will continue to be a stream of students entering college with the traditional beliefs of Christian absolutism. If, as seems certain, social science continues to advocate cultural relativism, the traditional conflict between views that has confronted college students in the past will also continue. Thus many students will continue to be caught between the demands of their Christian upbringing and the social sciences they encounter in college.

This dilemma is painful for many. It is especially so for those who are most capable and attentive to these issues.

There are those who are sure that the opposing side in this conflict has little or nothing to offer, and these individuals retain a stereotyped view of their opponents' position. For such people, the wall which separates probably cannot be crossed. Nevertheless, I have found that there are those of each persuasion who suspect that there is benefit in comparing positions, who are unwilling to adopt dogma without examination, and are equally unwilling to stereotype.

The concerns of Christian absolutists about cultural relativity are neither limited to intellectuals nor of recent origin. I still have a vivid childhood memory of an uneducated Sunday school teacher in a fundamentalist church who warned the class about those teachers who teach that truth is relative. In working with college students, I encounter many who in various ways have been caught in the competing contentions of Christian absolutism and cultural relativity. They are often unable to articulate the conflict in the terms I am using here. Yet when this material is presented to them, they recognize it as the basic conflict they are experiencing, and they become very interested in following this exploration to its conclusion.

The foregoing discussion suggests an interpretation about each side which will later be developed. That Christian absolutism can at times be dangerous has been well-documented. People who believe themselves to be armed with a special message from God are sometimes willing to wreak havoc on others. They may be very sure that their work is of God, though others are not persuaded. Such absolutists are usually not restrained by the opinions of others. Such people may do great damage. Yet to see them as the logical outcome of the committed Christian's absolutist faith is unpersuasive. There are too many Christian abso-lutists who exhibit none of these dangerous tendencies.

But cultural relativity is not immune to becoming dangerous either. Social groups need the definitions of reality that provide the members with a code of truth and morality. The problem of overly rigid norms and roles has often been analyzed in sociology, and students have felt liberated in the process. Yet the problem today often is not overly rigid beliefs and morality but an absence of any meaningful beliefs and norms—what is termed *anomie*. Sociology has tended to focus on debunking belief systems while ignoring the study of the process by which necessary social values can be developed and maintained.

In conclusion, the issue between Christian absolutists and cultural relativists is relevant to Christians, social scientists, secular humanists, the educated in general, and society itself. There is good reason to study and consider it whatever one's viewpoint. The cultural division is costly for both sides and painful for many individuals. If there are potential benefits to be gained from the study of the dispute, there is justification for doing so.

The basic purpose in examining the two sides of this issue is to do for both sides what Max Weber once said was the specific function of science: "to ask questions about those things which convention makes self-evident."[32] It does require of author and reader a willingness to ask such questions about one's own views as well as those of the other side. In doing this we can at least understand better what each side is walling in and walling out. But perhaps much more than this can be achieved.

2

The Challenge of Science

War is a science, Pippin.
That takes half the fun out of it right there.
—Roger O. Harrison

"Psychology is scientific fact while Christianity is only belief!" My friend—a Christian minister and an absolutist—made this declaration emphatically. His manner and tone of voice, as well as his words, conveyed most clearly the challenge science poses to Christianity. He assumed as an unassailable fact that there is a firm, proven basis for science while Christianity was believed to rest its case upon an unproven base. He was an uneasy absolutist: committed to the Christian position, he could not escape the underlying sense that scientists really know the truth that they affirm, while Christians can only hope theirs is so. The implications of this assumption are far more important than the debates over particular issues of dispute between science and Christianity.

William Pollard, a physicist and priest who has written concerning science and the Christian faith, stated the challenge in this way:

> The mid-twentieth century is an age which axiomatically grants truth and validity to scientific knowledge, but equally axiomatically discounts religious knowledge as mere opinion. This presents no problem to one conformed to the pervading convictions of his age. But to me, for whom the new range of reality I had come to know as a Christian was just as valid and substantial as the range of reality I knew as a physicist, it was a problem which acquired a primary importance to my thinking.[1]

Pollard reported that he had often been asked how as a physicist he could be a believing Christian. "It has often struck me," he wrote, "that had God given it to me to live in the sixth century or even the twelfth instead of the twentieth, the situation would have been exactly reversed."[2] In those periods the conventional idea would have been that Christianity was factual but physics a matter of speculation. Pollard, an advocate of science who remained an active physicist, conveys that a major element in the power of science to be convincing is found in the traits of contemporary culture. It is this that makes it seem so factual and not the inherent persuasiveness of its work. His contention is supported by cultural relativity. What science reports as true is convincing in large part because our culture reinforces the idea that it is the reliable way of knowing. To recognize the role of culture is not to disparage the power of science. But it does put it into a different perspective: it can cause us to look beyond the conventional view that our culture reassures us is reliable and examine the subject more carefully.

The Importance of Epistemology

Science's claim that it is a superior way of knowing is buttressed by its method of establishing knowledge. This involves us in the subject of epistemology—the study of how we know what we know. When science is presented as a way of knowing, it seems to exhibit a clear superiority over alternative ways. If you ask a scientist how a person can have confidence that science knows what it says it knows, the scientist can give a clear statement that makes sense. Furthermore, descriptions of scientific knowledge can be presented so that they are understandable even to a child.

Science is confident that it knows how it knows! Its way of knowing is based upon empirical data, carefully measured variables, and explicit methods of research that can be replicated. This means that the way of knowing is clear and that it is always supposed to be open to proof or disproof. That is, the methods of any research project are to be made explicit so that other scientists will know exactly what was done and can, if they desire, duplicate the experiment to see if the results are the same. Critical examination and replication are encouraged as basic components of the scientific method.

If, on the other hand, a Christian is asked how Christians know what they say they know, one will not be given such a clear and convincing statement. An exhortation on the necessity of having faith may be given. Or there may be a testimony. If the person asked has been interested in apologetics—the study that specializes in explaining the ways by which Christian truth can be proven—an elaborate explanation may be given. But there will not be a short, clear, simple explanation that will sensibly answer the question.

Christians, furthermore, usually assert truths but discourage critical examination. This is not to say that Christians do not think about the way they know what they know. The many Christian scholars who devote themselves to apologetics often produce impressive work, but to date they have failed to provide the simple, clear-cut epistemology comparable to the scientific method.

This is not an argument against the factuality of Christian truth. It does not intend to suggest that science is likely to be true and Christianity false. It is to point to a basic difference between the two ways of knowing that gives science an advantage in any epistemological struggle with Christianity.

The Christian may sing with spirit and conviction the chorus that has been so popular:

> I serve a risen savior
> He's in the world today.
> I know that he is living
> Whatever men may say . . .
>
> You ask me how I know he lives,
> He lives within my heart.

As rousing as such music may be, it does not provide a convincing epistemology for Christian faith. The subjective Christian experience is extremely important. But can it justifiably be considered as evidence for the resurrection of Jesus as the song seems to claim? Why are Christian claims often made on such a questionable base? I suspect that it is because of the nature of our church activities. Traditional Christianity seeks to build faith, not questions. Not surprisingly, most Christian groups do not encourage the critical questioning that is a fundamental part of science's approach. The education in absolutist schools has been described as an "intellectual transfer rather than an intellectual quest. Choice, doubt, suspended judgment, and dissent are excluded."[3] In a skeptical age, science seems appealingly open-minded, while traditional Christianity often appears to be narrow, closed-minded, and defensive. As a consequence, the challenge of science is formidable. In our culture it has the highest standing as a way of knowing, and it can articulate its methods very well. When the social scientist draws upon cross-cultural studies to illustrate the role of cultural relativity, people who know about it are likely to be convinced because of the epistemological standing of science itself. This poses a powerful challenge to Christian interpretations.

Science's Disclaimers

Social scientists often explicitly disclaim any intention of challenging religion. In the sociology of religion this means that the author of a text may claim that there is no connection between sociological questions and questions of religious truth. Johnstone, for example, wrote that he was "not going to be able nor even want to speak about the truth or falsity of religion."[4] The sociology of religion, he states, has a "nonevaluative intent" concerning religion. But Johnstone also adds that sociology utilizes the scientific method, requiring "evidence as opposed to hearsay, opinion, intuition, or common sense and involving procedures that others can verify and replicate."[5]

These "product disclaimers" may seem reasonable to people who have taught social science. They have encountered students from absolutist backgrounds who are defensive toward any statement that appears to slight their Christian faith. Unaccustomed to having religion as a subject of critical analysis, they are disturbed with what they perceive as an attack upon their faith. In some instances they correctly perceive that an instructor is attacking Christianity. But they also may perceive as an attack what is, instead, the normal procedure in investigating and considering subject matter. The product disclaimer allows the professor to claim innocence for any charges that the subject material might be an attack upon religion.

But is it accurate to claim that sociology has nothing to say and, furthermore, is not even interested in questions concerning the truth of religion? There are questions in the sociology of religion not related to such questions of truth. But the whole subject cannot be so disassociated. The sociology of knowledge raises basic questions about all kinds of knowledge, including religious knowledge. Any survey course in the sociology of religion is simply ignoring a very important area of sociological thought if it precludes these questions.[6]

Sociology textbooks regularly juxtapose the disclaimer with assertions about the objectivity of science that, at least by implication, questions all other ways of knowing. The quotations already cited from Johnstone do this by the reference to science's use of "evidence" as opposed to the ways of knowing that are used by religion. Notice Elizabeth Nottingham's emphasis:

> Even though it would be impossible to demonstrate that the analysis of religion by science is universally beneficial, it can be argued that the long run consequences of scientific study are beneficial, whereas a continuance of ignorance and bias is in the long run harmful.[7]

Such statements make their point quite clearly: science is a reliable way of ascertaining fact, but religion is at best a matter of ignorance and bias. The assumed superiority of scientific epistemology over other forms is clear. The authors assert that science knows how it knows while religion does not. The sociologist is portrayed as being above the fray. No attacks are made because none are needed. The sociologist has simply asserted that science's knowledge is sure and all other ways of knowing are unsure. The surgeon—so to speak—has denied any need to operate while surgically removing the heart of the patient!

The end result is that the scientific challenge remains, even though sociologists may deny that any challenge has occurred. The sociologist is then ahead of the student. The challenge remains in the basic assumptions of the subject, even though they are denied in the explicit writings. Earlier sociologists examined issues relating to the sociology of religion without any such disclaimers of interest in factuality. Their writings often did call into question matters of basic interest to Christians. Because of this, evangelical authors such as Dyrness, in analyzing the threat of sociology to Christianity, usually focus upon early figures such as Durkheim, Marx, and Weber.[8]

Is the Scientific Challenge Invincible?

For a long time many people have believed that the scientific challenge would destroy traditional Christian belief. As discussed briefly in the first chapter, not only has this failed to occur, but in any forseeable future there is no evidence that Christian belief will diminish or wither away. What *is* a reasonable prediction is that there will continue to be a running conflict between Christian absolutists and science.

But if science's challenge is so powerful, why has it been unable to overwhelm absolutist Christianity? Science has, certainly, its appealing epistemology. But it is not a matter of interest to most Americans. The National Commission on Excellence in Education expressed concern at the declining interest in the study of science. Educated Americans, it reported, know far less science now than they did in the past, in spite of the needs of our technological society. The commission was concerned about "a growing chasm between a small scientific and technological elite and a citizenry ill-informed, indeed uninformed, on issues with a scientific component."[9] The importance of science in our culture is not matched by either widespread knowledge or interest. Most people seem to agree with Pippin that anything that is a science could not be much fun.

Science does have an impact upon all of us through the technology that produces consumer goods. We clearly appreciate these goods. The automobile, television, and computer are examples of the long list of products that provide us with power and a sense of mastery. We associate this mastery with our well-being. The technology of the hospital of today is believed to be so powerful that people are often shocked and disbelieving when told that the staff has done all that it can to aid a patient who then dies. "There must be something that can be done!" is a familiar response. Is it not because health care technology is so powerful that we are shocked to encounter its limits? The breakthroughs in knowledge that make the technology possible and the products themselves give us a sense of mastery in the universe that becomes a part of our collective interpretation. It is reasonable to see science as powerful even if it is uninteresting.

The science that has produced the technology of powerful, productive machinery and the intricate stock of medical techniques has also produced the horror of weapons through which a balance of terror has emerged. Ernest Becker has reminded us that without access to the power of modern technology, primitive peoples still used their available knowledge trying to control their situations. Though such knowledge was often ineffective, one result of its lack of power was that it did not portend the destruction of whole societies—a fear we experience with today's technology.[10] Nevertheless, an argument for the abandonment of science is not seriously considered. We continue to hope that the terror it has made possible can be effectively dealt with in some way. We accept science because of its power when applied to invention and production—while remaining uninterested in it as a subject.

But there are other aspects of science that also probably prevent it from being invincible. A second major factor is related to the desire for meaning found in all cultures. Science is unable to provide this. The scientific method seeks to identify factors (called "variables") that are related to each other. The relationship determines which variable causes the other. For example, a drop in temperature below zero degrees centigrade may be said to affect water so that it becomes ice. This is a causal relationship. Beyond the vast complexities of all sciences, whether natural or social, all findings involve the discovery of variables that cause changes in other variables. This is true whether a particular research project seeks the conditions that cause a virus to multiply or a type of metal to withstand a greater impact. In learning how to relate conditions and identify causes, the scientist learns to control matters previously not controllable.

What is lacking in this is any explanation of meaning. When successful in identifying a cause, the scientist can explain under what conditions a certain event will occur. The scientist thus answers the question as to why something happens by explaining under what conditions it will occur. What the scientist cannot do is explain why something happens in the sense of the meaning of the event. Bernard Lown expressed it this way: "While science may help explain how a virus multiplies, it leaves unanswered why a tear is shed."[11]

This is not meant to be a criticism of science. It is intended to serve as an explicit reminder of what the interpretations of scientific work tend to obscure: science is in essence the establishing of a cause and effect relationship between variables. It cannot do anything more than this no matter how many applications it finds for that information. When science is associated with a myth of knowledge, it is distorted. As productive as it has been in many areas, when stripped of the myth, it is a search for variables that are related.

About social science, Babbie writes:

> Social science can assist us in knowing only what is and why. It can be used to address the question of what ought to be only when there is agreement on the criteria for deciding what's better than something else. Furthermore, this seldom occurs.[12]

In other words, the interpretation and evaluation can only occur if there is already a consensus of values. Does this indicate that it is a mistake to look for meaning? Is meaning only an illusion left over from past epochs of ignorance? If something must be discoverable by science to exist, then meaning—because it cannot be scientifically discovered—would be considered an illusion. However, it can be empirically established that people perform better and more efficiently when they find an activity to be meaningful. The functioning of the organism is effected by the ascription of meaning in the consciousness of the individual. Behavior that is not meaningful is harmful and alienating. When meaninglessness is prevalent, it is destructive to a society. This is true in all cultures. Indeed, a function of culture is the imputation of systems of meaning for its members. Meaning is thus an important aspect in the quality of the life of the human.[13] In this sense, meaning is a scientifically verifiable phenomenon.

Meaning systems are characteristically very important to those who are part of them but irrational to those who are not. The Kwakiutl Indians have often been noted for their potlatches in which a member throws a social event and displays his qualities by giving gifts to others that are without economic value. The custom undoubtedly seems meaningless to us but was extremely meaningful to the traditional Kwakiutil. The Kwakiutil would undoubtedly find it difficult to understand the meaning many of us find in football.

We are left with the scientifically verifiable fact that meaning systems are an important part of culture and are important to the functioning of both individuals and society. What we cannot do is establish meaning from descriptions of causality. We cannot develop meaning because we need meaning. We cannot make ourselves enjoy potlatches. What is sometimes called the "sickness of our age" is a pervasive sense of meaninglessness. People who are afflicted know that they suffer a sense of meaninglessness, but this insight does not produce meaning. The cause and effect systems of science seem to be incapable of dealing with issues of meaning. The social sciences could become more involved with research that would seek to explore how systems develop meaning, but this has been of little interest to the discipline thus far. Even if sociologists were to make such an effort, it would be to identify those situations that cause meaning systems to develop. It would not provide meaning itself.

A third factor is that science is not invincible when it goes beyond its data and asserts that it is more than a method for finding cause and effect; when it contends that it is the only way of knowing; and when it asserts that all it knows is all that there is to know. Science is not invincible, in other words, when it is itself absolutist. Of course, not all scientists assert this. If stated in this way, most scientists probably would deny it. But it does occur. Carl Sagan's television series, *Cosmos*, was critically acclaimed by scientists and non-scientists alike as an important vehicle for teaching lay people about science. In it, Sagan seemed to assert that the material world apprehendable by scientific method is the sum of all existence. He declared: "The cosmos is all that is or ever was or ever will be."[14] Mr. Sagan's science, indeed, takes on the characteristics of religion as was noted by Richard Baer in the *Wall Street Journal:*

> "Some part of our being," states Mr. Sagan, "knows that this [the cosmic ocean] is where we came from." And the cosmos, he continues, is not just our place of origin. It is also our final goal. "We long to return [to it]. And we can, because the cosmos is also within us." Simply substitute the terms "God" or "Christ" for "cosmos," and the religious character of these statements becomes clear.[15]

Clearly Sagan went beyond his data. In spite of the rhetoric of empiricism, there is no empirical referent in these statements. I suspect that most scientists would not accept this enthusiasm for the "cosmos" that Sagan displayed. Yet that which he displayed so forcefully in the series is not unusual in science. In fact, the support given to this series should embarrass the empirical scientist who recognizes both the powers and limits of the method.

When science attempts to become "the" way of knowing rather than "a powerful" way of knowing, it has a tendency to make assertions about itself that, though enthusiastic, are unsubstantiated. Sociology itself was subject to the enthusiasm of an early authority, Auguste Comte, who attempted to form a religion of science. Such efforts have never had any prospect of success and in retrospect appear to be foolish. Science as a substitute for religion is too vulnerable to be taken seriously. It is too devoid of any inner consistency within its own structure of concepts. Yet, to appraise it for what it is—a study of cause and effect—is to see it as a powerful tool which alters the lives and experiences of all of us. But it is a tool and not a guide. It may be that the writing of a scientist will provide superior insight about matters of meaning. If it does, however, the superior wisdom will not be scientific, it will not be validated by scientific research, and it will not meet the criteria of science. To realize the failure of science as a guide in the meaning of life is not to diminish its power: it puts it into a useful perspective.

There have been some who have been so immersed in science and so hopeful of what future discoveries could do for people that science became for them a meaning for their lives. But this has been satisfactory for only a few. At some point most recognize what a colleague of mine expressed when we had assembled to pay tribute to another colleague who had died, "There is nothing in sociology which can help us in a time like this." This may sound like an emotional illustration from a sermon, but is it not also realistic? Sociologists, social scientists, and all scientists at some point would do well to recognize that science, though it may be extremely valuable and impressive, seems unable to provide the insights on the meaning of existence for which people hope.

In questions of meaning, whatever we can know with confidence—if there is anything—must be derived from some other source. Scientific knowledge may be invincible in its area of application. But it also is not relevant to some areas. When it tries to become an all-encompassing authority it simply becomes mystical, speculative, and ultimately foolish. Thus, its challenge to the faith of the Christian absolutist may not be as important as has been thought. The growth of Christian absolutists in numbers and influence has been contrary to the expectations of social scientists who have believed secularization to be an irreversible process.

Yet, if Christians seek to challenge science in its domain of cause and effect relationships, they may fritter away their resources in a futile battle. On the other hand, if they concentrate on their own domain, understand their own ways of knowing, and seek to maintain an open relationship with science, they may find that the challenges of science are helpful rather than harmful. In such a stance, they also will be in a position to challenge when science wanders out of its domain.

To summarize, the scientific challenge is powerful in its method of knowing and in its reputation as a method for establishing fact. As such it is a formidable challenge to any other method of knowing. While science cannot successfully function as a religion, it can mount a strong challenge, since its basic premises are validated by empirical research. It is unable now and probably will be unable in the future to successfully overwhelm Christian absolutism. People are not sufficiently interested in it, and it is unable to provide the meaning in life that is a more immediate concern. What does seem likely is that there will be a continuing struggle between these two ways of knowing. As is true of any such struggle, many people will expend time, energy, and resources in the process of the contentions.

3

The Gauntlet Taken Up

Always be prepared to give an answer to everyone who asks you
for the hope that you have. But do this with gentleness and respect.
—2 Peter 3:15, NIV

Though the challenge of science to religion has been present for a very long
time—Galileo's initial impact was almost four centuries ago—a mood has in
recent years become evident among Christian absolutists to aggressively con-
front this and other challenges. Absolutists who have been content to teach in
the churches and colleges and to write in their journals now advocate taking up
the gauntlet hurled by the relativists and carrying the contest into the public
arena. Jerry Falwell has captured the attention of the news media in the decade
of the '80s. As is characteristic of a charismatic figure, he has engendered both
support and antagonism from various sectors of American society.

Robert Zwier attributed this new mood to the success of "born-again politics"
in the 1980 elections.[1] This impact increased in the 1984 election.[2] Whatever
the fate of the public mood on such political involvement, the issues that
occasioned the rise of the debate will continue. They preceeded the current
political involvements, and they will be around after the public mood has
changed.

Edward Dobson has charged that social relativism, moral decadence, and
unbridled materialism provide "undeniable testimony" that our society has
turned away from God.[3] Jerry Falwell has usually defined his position around
specific issues such as abortion, armament, anti-ERA, and pro-Israel policies.
But the underlying importance of the issues of absolutism and cultural relativity
have sometimes been made explicit: "Students are told that there are no
absolutes and that they are to develop their own value systems . . . Humanists
believe that man is his own god and that moral values are relative, that ethics are
situational."[4]

Falwell concludes that "the demise of [Christian] liberalism and the dissolution of its impact on American society" stems from a lack of belief in "absolute
truth."[5] Whatever the specific issue he takes up, an underlying cause is traced to

this destructive relativism. And Falwell intends to take up the issues. "We have the opportunity to formulate a new beginning for America in this decade," he has written.[6] He issued a call for Christians to move "out of the pew and into the precinct."[7]

But Falwell is by no means alone. Tim LaHaye has called for "an army of moral activists" to register Christians to vote, to help the campaign of "pro-moral candidates," run for office, and expose the "amoral" candidates and incumbents.[8] LaHaye sees the "poor, the refugees, and the troubled" as "victims of humanism's libertine concepts."[9]

Francis Schaeffer also took up the gauntlet. The worldview of science that he described as a "material-energy chance" concept is, in his view, completely impossible to reconcile with the Christian concepts.[10] No synthesis is possible. The scientific view produces what Schaeffer called "sociological law."[11] It is relativistic, and it is destructive. Christians "must not only take the necessary legal and political stands, but must practice all the possible Christian alternatives simultaneously with taking stands politically and legally."[12] Among the alternatives is civil disobedience:

> It is time we consciously realize that when any office commands what is contrary to God's Law it abrogates its authority.[13]
> And if we do not practice the bottom line of civil disobedience on the appropriate level, when the state has abrogated its authority, we are equally not living under the Scripture.[14]

An article in the *New York Times,* typical of many such reports, has stated that "in Plano, Texas, teachers no longer ask students their opinions because to do so, they have been told, is to deny absolute right and wrong."[15] Teaching techniques that involve role playing and discussion have been attacked because they are considered to imply a lack of absolute right and wrong.[16] Whether the Plano teachers have been "straightened out" or "unreasonably intimidated" is not the point here. Every issue gets stated in various ways, and one can always find extreme statements to justify the mistakes of the other side. But it is clear that absolutists are challenging the status quo. Rightly or wrongly, change is being sought.

It is evident, therefore, that Christian absolutists are not contending for change only within their own buildings. They are voicing their positions in public on an array of social issues. They are challenging established ways of doing things and are increasingly willing to consider the use of civil disobedience in specific issues. The gauntlet has been taken up. They are choosing a collision course.

There are still many who believe Christians should stay out of the political arena. The response of the activists is that Christians have a right, like any special interest group, to contend for their views. In response to the charge that such activism is a violation of church and state separation, Jerry Falwell and others respond very precisely. Falwell has described the Moral Majority as being neither a political party nor a religious organization. It does not "believe that individuals or organizations that disagree [with it] belong to an immoral minority." It is "a platform for religious and nonreligious Americans who share moral values to address their concerns in these areas."[17]

For espousing this position, Falwell has been criticized. But this insistence that there is a basic right of all Americans—including Christians—to organize and express their points of view for the purpose of influencing governmental action seems well-supported. It seems difficult to challenge Charles Colson's simple response to Pat Robertson's announced interest in being a presidential candidate: "He has just as much right to run as anyone else."[18] The participation of special interest groups in government is part of the basic American process of giving and withholding the "consent of the governed." Whether it is an effective long-term strategy for the mission of Christians is a different and more difficult question.

Those who support the activists in taking up the gauntlet express a determination to increase the effectiveness of their participation. No longer content to shake their heads at a society that they perceive as decaying, they are moving into the public arena. This effort is certainly not limited to the fundamentalists. As Ron Sider notes, "From conservative fundamentalists to radical evangelicals, involvement in public life is now a mandate rather than a sin."[19] Is it legitimate to be concerned at the emergence of religious-political movements? Historically, it has been argued, they have been authoritarian. In the context of American pluralism, however, the denial of the right of participation or attempts to inhibit groups such as the Moral Majority and Liberty Foundation would seem to be inconsistent with the basic tenets of American government.

The Fate of the Challenge to Secularization

Will the aggressive stance of absolutists be effective in the long run? The mistaken prediction that science would lead to a fully secularized society was discussed in an earlier chapter. Yet Peter Berger's analysis in *The Sacred Canopy* may still provide us with useful insight. The progress of secularization, he contended, would be difficult to defend against "in the measure that the outside world is atttractive."[20] It would seem that Berger wrote these words just about the time that the world took a turn that made it less attractive to a great many people. The world after Vietnam, Watergate and other corruptions; the energy crisis; and the progressing nuclear arms race did not produce a world that people found to be attractive. The resurgence of traditional Christianity to an aggressive rather than defensive posture is clearly aided by the loss of confidence in the attractiveness of the secular world.

It seems reasonable to anticipate a secular world which will continue to be unattractive. The Second World War proved that it did not end wars any more than the first. Hitler's cruelty to Jews has turned out not to be an isolated event. Cambodia, Argentina, Guatemala, and Afghanistan are but a few of the places to experience official murder. Sometimes it is reported in news articles, but usually it is given little attention. But we cannot always look the other way. The disappeared people and the pictures of sprawled bodies are recurring events in a bloody, suffering, disoriented world.

In 1967, Berger may well have identified the dynamics of the process even though his assumptions of a world that would remain attractive, and thus secularized did not come about. By 1974 he also perceived some failures of the world that he had not noted earlier. In his book, *Pyramids of Sacrifice*, he cited evidence in both the western societies and in Marxist countries of a failure of materialism. The evidence was not simply a failure of economics in which not enough goods were produced. Rather, it was a basic failure of material things to provide for human fulfillment. It posed, he wrote, "some serious questions for the view that contemporary man is embarked on an inexorable and irreversible course of secularization."[21]

It is now possible to chart the result of this shift in thinking. Greeley had just published *Unsecular Man*, asserting continuing strength of Christian world-views, when Berger's later book was published. The explosion of fundamentalism discussed by Jerry Falwell in *The Fundamentalist Phenomenon* was underway. No longer did the traditionalists need to huddle together to protect the faith. The word now was to attack wrongs in the secular world and rescue it from destruction by reorienting it. It was, in Falwell's words, "to formulate a new beginning for America."[22]

If it was, as Falwell contended, the "inherent lack of absolute truth" that led to the "demise of [religious] Liberalism and the dissolution of its impact on American society," then the objective was clear: absolutism must be restored.[23] The accommodation of Christians to the cultural relativity prevalent in the secular world has prevailed in some American Christian denominations, but these denominations have dwindled in membership. The absolutists, having lost the controversies of the 1920s, retreated to rebuild their churches and organizations.[24] Today they have regained their strength and are reasserting their mission.

The gauntlet has been taken up. The challenges of science are accepted and science is, in return, also challenged. Cultural relativity as a factor in knowing is rejected and is considered to be a basic cause of all societal problems. Only the absolutism of Christian knowledge, it is contended, can provide the foundation upon which America or any society can stand. The projections of increasing secularization, according to the absolutists, can now be dismissed as wrong.

Other Challenges to Secularization

The challenge posed by those who identify themselves as fundamentalists, their increased assertiveness, and their increased confidence in their role of redirecting American society is paralleled by other movements. These others are similarly willing to challenge the conventional views of a secular society. They share the idea that freedom of religion is not limited to the practice of conventional religion in conventional church buildings. They believe that it is not un-American to attempt to spread their values by publicly challenging the ideas of the society. They also are "taking up the gauntlet" against a scientific, secularizing society. They share little else. The following four examples are given as illustration rather than as a systematic review of such efforts.

Marxist sociologist Richard Quinney has written that there is "a theology emerging inspired by the prophetic Marx."[25] Marxism has failed, he noted, "to provide us with the symbols that relate to questions of the infinite and eternal that we apprehend in our lives."[26] Indeed, he wrote that "the orthodox Marxist notion that religion is solely the 'opium of the people,' the tool of the oppressor, cannot be sustained by subsequent historical evidences."[27] Marx, he believes, was also wrong in another aspect of his analysis of religion:

> Marx, in his own rationalism and antireligious fervor, underestimated the force of religion in shaping revolutionary consciousness and in evoking action. He not only undercalculated its durability, but he also overlooked its "potential for catalyzing political and cultural transformation."[28]

This new theology is, according to Quinney, a "rediscovery of the eschatological dimension in both Marxism and theology."[29] It is a rejection of the Marxist materialism as a sufficient explanation by which to live. It is an attempt to add to Marxism a theological explanation, but it does not represent a rejection of Marxism as such. There is in this an unwillingness to accept conventional Maxist definitions of reality, considering them inadequate without a theological component.

Second, Hunter identifies evangelicals who have aligned with the New Class of secularists reflecting "left liberal political values and ideology."[30] They are best identified by two magazines, *Sojourners* and *The Other Side*, which are published in Washington, D.C., and Philadelphia respectively. They combine liberal social ideas with assertive Christian commitment. Their efforts are not in the classical liberal mode of accommodation with the prevailing culture. They are challenging the social system in support of the poor, the disinherited, and the dispossessed. They support the peace movement by advocating disarmament rather than armament. They engage in civil disobedience. Perhaps illustrative of this approach is the attempt to make use of church buildings as sanctuaries to shelter illegal aliens who have fled the turmoil of Latin America.

This activism is Christian. These are not the stereotypical secular activists often found in the earlier civil rights movement whose motivations were often based less on Christian commitment than a humanistic concern for social equality. These people are Christians first, and their commitment to Christianity is expressed in their challenges to conventional Americanism.

The third example is that expressed by the title of Harvey Cox's book, *Turning*

East. One Sunday afternoon, he found two Hare Krishna devotees on his doorstep. The realization that a surprising number of American youths had been taking up oriental religious practices led to his decision to study what was happening in this phenomenon. In doing so, Cox began as "more an observer than a participant" but soon found himself very involved. He believed that this unexpected involvement was a result of some unusual and unrecognized personal need. He soon discovered that his experience was not unusual. Many of the people involved did so for personal reasons that had little to do with the official teachings of the religion.[31] What Cox had learned about Oriental religious traditions "seemed to have little connection with what was happening."[32] He found far more people involved and more variety of movements than he had expected.

> There is something new about the present situation. In previous decades, interest in Oriental philosophy was confined mostly to intellectuals and was centered largely on ideas, not on devotional practices. There is no evidence that Emerson (who wrote about Oriental religion) ever sat in a full lotus. Today, on the other hand, not only are large numbers of people who are in no sense "intellectuals" involved, but they appear more interested in actual religious practices than in doctrinal ideas.[33]

Though interest in this turn to the Orient seems to have waned, it has not disappeared. Americans who participate demonstrate a willingness to accept unconventional ideas as being objectively true to an unusual degree, to accept religious views that have neither empirical nor traditional support. These are not people so conditioned by scientific thinking that they are unable to believe in non-empirical reality. They are quite able to accept ways of knowing that have no scientific-empirical support. Some have referred to the rise of the diverse range of religious movements as an "age of the spirit." Not all of one stripe, they range from fundamentalist Christian to Hare Krishna, and from far right to far left. It has been seen by some to have originated as a reaction to the turmoil of the Vietnam War-flower child area. Disillusioned with all institutions, it was said, people were adrift. Thus many are said to have found religion to be a "turn-on."

The fourth example is of a different nature. Kathleen Agena has cited evidence to support her contention that a new wave of interest in "magical beings" and "enchanted realms" has appeared. She cites these occurrences in television, films, art, and in both popular and serious literature. She finds it "startling" to discover this "fascination with mystical symbols and motifs that hark back to notions of an enchanted universe and to the hierarchical social order of the middle ages."[34]

What is the cause of this trend? "The expressions of fantasy that we're seeing in the culture are arising like antibodies to fight the disease of sterile rationality that prevails in our society."[35] This trend may, of course, be nothing but a fad. It is always easy to read too much importance into short-term shifts in interests. Yet her examples are diverse, and each represents a decided turn. It would also be a mistake to ignore the possible implications. It may be one more category of evidence that human society has not entered the scientific age of rationality as had been expected. It represents, at the very least, areas of culture in which there is an unwillingness to submit to the ideas and images of science.

This range of four examples, while being notable for its diversity, also shares a commonality: There is a common rejection of the scientific-empirical-secular way of knowing as the only real way of knowing. Whatever the explanation for this era, it came at a time when the consensus of intellectuals was that the rising level of education in our age was rapidly producing a secular worldview that would reject the non-objective superstitions (i.e., religion in its various forms) for objective-empirical-relativistic ways of knowing (i.e., science).

The news media have focused a considerable amount of attention to these movements. Yet, when all of them are considered together, they comprise a small number compared to the people involved in the rise of fundamentalism. Whether the news media continue to give attention to absolutist Christianity is not of crucial importance, because it has developed the organizational structure to carry itself forward. The alternative movements are instructive for what they indicate about the receptiveness of people to non-scientific beliefs. They are also instructive for what they indicate about the willingness of people to believe in movements that have little or no cultural support in the society. But the major impact on society in the forseeable future is likely to be in fundamentalism.

The Future of the Fundamentalists' Assault

If fundamentalists are viewed in terms of the stereotypes of the past, they will be incorrectly assessed. In his appraisal of fundamentalism, Jerry Falwell cited a number of weaknesses that have long been evident in the past. Considered as a group, he wrote, these weaknesses have resulted in a quarrelsome, divisive, and isolationist pattern that has led to a stagnation of previous surges in evangelistic success. Falwell calls for a new spirit that will produce "a generation of gentlemanly Fundamentalists who love equally the truth of God's Word and the people in whose lives it must be applied."[36]

Whether these attitudes—that have divided and crippled efforts in the past— will prevail again remains to be seen. Fundamentalists have recently experienced a period of growth with Falwell citing Towns' research to show that in 1979 twenty churches—most of which were fundamentalist—had an average Sunday school attendance weekly of 2,700–15,000. Ten years earlier, Towns had identified only eight such churches.[37] Oral Roberts University and Liberty University, as well as the older Bob Jones University, are sizeable institutions even in this age of large campus populations. The assumption that this surge will self-destruct is not warranted by any evidence other than projections from the past. When other outreaches of fundamentalism such as the Christian schools and television-radio programming are added to this, it is quite clear that there is a large-scale attempt to have an impact upon society.

The ease with which the movement can be caricatured may be misleading. The television fundamentalists who promise miracles and plead for money are similar to the "sawdust circuit." But fundamentalists come in many styles. It is clear that a large segment of America is responding. Sociologists do well to look not only at the caricatures but also at the range of people who are active in fundamentalist movements.

As a sociologist now teaching in an area that is clearly part of the Bible belt, I have observed the change in students over the past decade. Class lectures on the assumptions of science once were received with evident boredom. It was a ritual in the introduction of science to be endured before the real material of the subject began. The assumptions were labeled as such, but the students did not consider them questionable. The self-evident factuality of the assumptions was considered already settled. That has changed. Students often raise points and discuss the validity of the assumptions. I do not mean that they are attacking the assumptions. Rather, it is that the assumptions are perceived to be worth thinking about. The students are usually willing to accept science's assumptions, but they do not accept them out of an unquestioned respect for science as being a way to sure knowledge.

A second change is that there has been an increasing number of students who readily identify themselves as born-again Christians. Admittedly they come in a wide array of styles, yet the most prevalent is not the "religious nut" of the past. Every class I have taught in recent years has had several persons who have identified themselves as born-again Christians. It has been several years since any have been obnoxious about it; a decade ago such students were fewer in numbers but more likely to be defensive and contentious. I do not know how prevalent this change is, or what the experience of other sociologists has generally been, but I have experienced a decided change among my students.

Another change is the willingness to accept alternative ways of knowing. In the past, Christian students were more interested in questioning the traditional beliefs, hoping to arrive at a justification of those beliefs by rationally thinking them through. To base belief on experiences that seemed to confirm one's faith was viewed as too subjective and therefore not reliable. The students with whom I have contact now are not as confident in the ability of rational thought to establish knowledge, nor are they as questioning of subjective experiences as a way of confirming truth. This is not to say that they are unaware of the psychological processes by which subjective experiences may express needs of the psyche rather than the truth of the universe. But, taking into allowance that which the behavioral sciences can potentially offer, they often seem to be able to place faith in their subjective experiences as ways to know truth.

In these personal experiences I find the changes in the characteristics of the students to be consistent with the statistical trends of the society. The old scientific and religious arguments have changed in how they are conducted. A quarter of a century ago, the criteria for the debate were usually those of the scientists. The anti-scientists were on the defensive from the beginning. This is not so often true now. The congruence of experience and published research indicates that the fundamentalists have sustained among a segment of society a plausibility for their positions, have increased confidence in their positions, and have resources now to take up the challenges posed by the sciences. The anticipated era when the assumptions of social science would be accepted as the way of knowing seems to have already peaked and is declining. Hunter is undoubtedly correct in his data that the fundamentalist view is still very much a minority view.[38] But it is an increasingly self-confident and assertive minority.

The evidence is clear that the gauntlet of science's challenge to religion has been accepted. Fundamentalist Christianity is demonstrating that a wide range of people, including a good number of the educated, are quite willing and able to place faith in ways of knowing that are not scientific. Further, the challenge is carried into the public arena where questions of government, law, and education are now subject to scrutiny and aggressive lobbying by representatives of the values of Christian fundamentalists. The expectation of a time close at hand when the basic way of knowing would be modeled after the scientific is nowhere in sight. Science has long been concerned with the lack of interest in and support for its efforts. The critically acclaimed television program, *Nova,* was produced in an effort to elicit popular support for science. Recent concerns for education as expressed through national reports have focused upon this lack of interest in science. Those producing the reports are attempting to sell a change on the basis of the national economy: if we do not produce more scientists we will lag behind other nations in the marketplace of goods and all be poorer for it. Science becomes necessary, according to this view, as the source of affluence, but not as a way of knowing for its own sake.

Science, of course, is too productive to diminish or disappear. Its benefits are too obvious. It is a way of establishing cause and effect that has altered our lives. We will not turn away from the age of science. But neither does science appear able to obliterate other ways of knowing. The prediction remains that the struggle of these two often separated and antagonistic ways of knowing will continue.

Part II
Cultural Relativity

4

The Case for Cultural Relativity

> There is nothing either good or bad
> But thinking makes it so.
> —Shakespeare, *Hamlet*

Although Christian absolutists believe relativity is responsible for the view that nothing is really good or bad, Shakespeare wrote *Hamlet* long before either social science or its concept of relativity existed. The concept of cultural relativity resulted from empirical field research and its use was intended to further our understanding of human culture and knowledge. In this chapter attention turns to the idea of just what cultural relativity is and what it is not, as used by social scientists.

The Development of the Concept

The early anthropologists of a century ago believed in a "cultural evolution in which a society's level of technology indicated its peoples' intellectual capacity and ethical development."[1] For them this meant that European and North American societies were superior on the evolutionary scale in every respect, while other societies were inferior. They regarded their own culture as more intelligent, more morally sensitive, and more culturally complex—representing the top level of the evolutionary ladder from which the lower primitives could be studied and compared. We were, presumably, the mature adults while the others were immature children.

This thinking represented an extreme ethnocentrism that later anthropologists and sociologists found to be erroneous. In 1906, William Graham Sumner published a work that attacked this view.[2] The research of the early twentieth century provided increasing evidence to support his attack. Evidence mounted that the so-called primitives possessed vast amounts of knowledge, were sensitive in every sense of the word, and sustained language systems which were equally as complex as those of the industrial nations. They could only be considered to possess lower evolutionary standing if the criteria were carefully

49

selected. This was, of course, what had unconsciously occurred. The anthropologists had previously assumed that a developed industrial society was superior because it was industrial and produced so much in the way of manufactured goods. If other standards of comparison were used—such as qualities of loyalty, care for family members, or respect for the natural environment—a very different ranking would have occurred.

Herskovitz pointed out, for example, that the Australian aborigines who have been considered to be among the most primitive had a kinship system "so complex that for many years it defied the attempts of students to analyze it." By comparison our language makes little distinction in kinship. "We do not even distinguish between paternal and maternal grandparents, or older or younger brothers, and call literally dozens of relatives by the same word, 'cousin.'"[3] By the standard of a meaningful kinship system, he concluded, we are underdeveloped.

If these peoples who had been considered to be primitive and simple were not simple at all, what did this mean? When it was discovered that they had vast amounts of complex knowledge and used language systems that employed complex verb tenses and nuances of meaning, the ranking of cultures by evolutionary criteria was discredited. The social scientists had been victimized by their own ethnocentrism. Assuming their own superiority, they had used their own ideas as the standard of judgment. By doing this they assured their conclusion that other cultures would be found to be inferior.

But ethnocentrism is not simply a matter of distorted thinking. It has an inherent logic. Indeed, it is a characteristic of culture that its own truths, norms, and values will be seen as self-evidently true. They will seem to be absolutes against which all foreign ideas—if any are known—can be judged. And when judged, the foreign ideas inevitably will seem to be inferior. The anthropologists were doing what the primitives themselves would also do—that is, see reality ethnocentrically.

There is no doubt that industrial technology is impressive. The American social scientists were not alone in thinking their culture to be superior because they had industrially manufactured goods from their homeland. The primitive people were enticed by the products of the technology. In later years, the transistor radio would capture the world just as in earlier years the primitive peoples were astounded by the items of power and "magic" produced in the factories of America and Europe.

The problem for the social scientist doing fieldwork was that ethnocentrism prevented the possibility of understanding accurately the society being studied. Successful research required some method by which ethnocentrism could be eliminated. This meant an emphasis upon learning to suspend judgment, to be empathetic toward the culture being studied, and to assume the role of a detached observer. It meant that every belief and norm had to be understood in terms of the culture in which it existed and not be compared to the culture of the researcher. An awareness of cultural relativity became a methodological require-ment.

As researchers utilized cultural relativism in their studies, a new kind of literature appeared. It portrayed societies with beliefs and norms quite different from those of the researchers' homelands yet the descriptions lacked ethno-centric judgments. To people who were accustomed to statements with obli-gatory evaluation, such nonevaluative reporting seemed to suggest approval. For writing in this manner, the social scientist was seen as a person of doubtful moral fiber. In defense—a defense still widely used in textbooks—the social scientist was said to use this viewpoint only in the professional role, distinct from the role of citizen where, presumably, the social scientist was just like everyone else. This was probably never totally convincing, and in retrospect, there is no reason why it should have been. Methods of work and one's personal life are not easily compartmentalized completely, though some people seem to accomplish it. The anthropologist who had observed various alternative sexual norms in a tribe was not likely to regard sexual norms in quite the same way as he had previously.

The lines that this new approach to anthropology had taken were inevitably going to be in conflict with Christian fundamentalists. Harriet Martineau had correctly anticipated this when she wrote in 1856, "The theological world cannot but hate a book which treats of theological belief as a transient state of the mind."[4] As long as the battle for truth was seen as that between good and bad, friend and enemy, the absolutist concept of truth was unchallenged. Similarly, the cultural evolutionists who saw American and Western European culture as the most advanced and best did not question their own assumptions, no matter where they traveled or what they studied.

The moment the anthropologists began to guard against ethnocentrism they challenged the conventional way of thinking. Such a challenge is always disturb-ing. If polygamy, for example, was to be viewed as "their way" and examined without evaluation, noting whatever advantages and disadvantages it posed in the daily life of the village, was this to suggest that there was no clear superiority of our monogamy over their polygamy? If there was no superiority, did this mean there was no objective moral standard? If morality is only someone's idea, it is then only a state of mind, and Martineau knew this would be disturbing.

Cultural relativity seemed to challenge the basic possibility that Christianity could be objectively true. James Hunter has identified three potential options in response to this challenge. One was to reject the claim of any religion that the content of its traditions were objectively true. A second possibility was to see all religions as true to the extent that they shared common core elements. The third option was to resist by "ignoring the plurality" and "affirming the veracity of one tradition and the illegitimacy of the others."[5]

The first alternative contends that relativity has established that revealed, objective truth is impossible. Though many may hold this view, it should be logically unacceptable because it begs the empirical question. If religious revelation of objective truth has occurred and is knowable, it exists. If it has not occurred, it does not exist.

The second view assumes that there is a common wisdom that is found in various religions. This is not a consequence of revelation but of common solutions to common questions. The solutions are true not because of their source but because they are verifiable. In this interpretation, for example, the biblical teaching that husbands should love their wives would be considered true, not because it has been revealed but because it "makes sense"—that is, it appeals to our collective understanding of the way things should be.[6] In this view, the claim of a religion to a unique status of revelation is denied. Religious truth is accepted as established only by a social process and has no unique status.

The third option was to ignore the issue of relativism, reject as false all alternative religions, and assert one's own religion to be objectively true. This is the option Christian absolutists have taken. It can be very workable, but it has some liabilities. It creates a defensiveness in many Christians. There remains a lingering, though often unconscious, suspicion that its assertions of absolute truth may not be the way things really are. Such doubts cannot be directly dealt with because the raising of such issues is taboo. So the doubts must be suppressed, creating a dogmatic assertiveness and uneasiness about any questioning of one's position. The dogmatic assertiveness is, for many, an unattractive attribute of Christian absolutism that impedes efforts at evangelism. Though absolutists may consider the advantages of this option to be obvious, its liabilities are also important.

It is only this third option that seems to allow for the Christian to retain the traditional faith. My contention, to be presented later in this book, is that there is a fourth option that is both empirically sound and consistent with Christian tradition. That is, the relativity of human knowledge need not, in itself, effect the issue of Christian truth. Indeed, it does so only if we think that it does.

Hunter concluded that by the period of 1890–1919 the leading theological thought had abandoned supernaturalism and accepted "the relativization and equalization of all religious belief systems."[7] Thus mainstream Protestantism had accepted the first two options that denied to Christianity any unique properties of being objectively true. It was, in other words, considered true but no more true than Buddhism. The fundamentalists emerged in reaction to this as a minority who insisted on the third option. Christianity, they contended, was completely true and all religious beliefs which differed were untrue. A set of books, The Fundamentals, produced in 1907, was distributed at no cost to any minister who requested a set. These books attempted to reassert this objective truthfulness of the Christian faith. Fundamentalism, deriving its name from that set of books, has attempted to meet the challenge of relativity by asserting its fundamental beliefs, rather than encountering the issues that cultural relativity has raised.

This consideration of options does not engage us in the basic epistemological question of relativity: If the relativity of all human knowledge is accepted, is it a necessary conclusion that we can never really know anything for sure? If relativity destroys knowledge, that would be tragic. Yet, the consideration of relativism should be based on evidence rather than on whether we like its consequences.

Cross-cultural research has developed a number of insights into the process by which we arrive at what we "know." Every child being socialized into a society learns a set of conventional interpretations of the world from people with whom they have contact.

> Thought and perception cannot take place without such a conventional perspective, for the intellect requires a tool kit of concepts, theories, standards of judgment, and the like if it is to operate at all.[8]

These basic concepts and ideas by which a person encounters the world are a "scaffolding of our thoughts."[9] It is not that individuals do not think their own thoughts; of course we do. But our thoughts use a priori assumptions, they use the conventional concepts and ideas, and they are shaped by the time and place where we live. If one lives securely in the boundaries of one's own culture, this tool kit provides a common basis for defining the truth. There have been some African tribes whose women cut open their lips and insert wooden objects until the lip becomes very large and extended. They consider these "platter lips" to be beautiful, though we consider them very grotesque and ugly. This difference of evaluation is not a matter of personal opinion. The beauty they see is the consequence of the culture to which they belong. So our view is also a consequence of our culture. It reflects for each the cultural "scaffolding" of thought.

Our readiness to disagree and disparage the beliefs and norms of those in a foreign culture seems justifiable if we lack cross-cultural experience. As anthropologists studied diverse cultures, they realized that simply to pronounce other views as erroneous prevented understanding and increased misunderstanding.

> It now became evident that philosophers with viewpoints other than one's own could not be viewed simply as living in error which it was unnecessary to explain; it now became apparent that each of the different points of view represented in the history of thought appeared, from within its own situation, to be in fact nothing other than the truth itself.[10]

If a philosophy seems to be self-evident truth to the philosopher but not to me, I may decide to simply condemn the other as erroneous. But there is another option: I may try to "'get inside' the strange culture, or historical period, or person to such a degree that the strangeness of the customs and the ways of thought of the subject is overcome."[11]

In doing this I may gain an understanding of what the philosopher is contending that is far more likely to provide insight. Far from destroying truth, Kaufman argues, this use of relativity allows a person "to develop broader and more comprehensive knowledge of himself and his world."[12] That is, by accepting the basic assumptions of relativity, I am motivated to understand the other person's particular situation more fully. In doing this I am more likely to gain understanding.

Melvin Herskovitz is the anthropologist whose work is most often cited concerning cultural relativisim. Until his death in 1963, his career had involved him in the major trends of the concept's development. His wife edited his papers, published in 1972, and they provide insights on the controversies surrounding this concept—including the early excesses and misguided attacks that had sometimes occurred.

First, Herskovitz was totally convinced that cultural relativity as a method of anthropological work was a necessity. Only when ethnocentrism was countered could the anthropologist begin to understand a culture and ask the kinds of scientific questions that needed to be investigated.

Second, he held that every culture is internalized into the personalities of its members, and it provides the crucially important interpretative scheme with which the individual member encounters and interprets the experiences of daily life. This is what Herskovitz called "enculturation." It is in the enculturation that the person "knows." Morality and truth are defined within the culture and experienced by the individual through this enculturation.

Third, Herskovitz was very disturbed that discussions of cultural relativity seemed to be so often restricted to morals, ethics, and values. This, he believed, threw "the problem at issue out of focus since it undercut(s) the enculturative fact in cultural learning in general." He pointed out that relativism applied in all areas including such matters as "judgments of time, space, and volume as well as conduct."[13] All perceptions are influenced by culture. If the full impact on all ways of knowing were examined, he believed, it would be helpful in understanding how reality is defined.

Fourth, once ethnocentric judgments have been held in check and the culture understood in its own right, Herskovitz was quite willing to make comparative evaluations of one culture with another. When he wrote of polygamy among the Dahomey, for example, he was quite comparative and evaluative. As the leading advocate of cultural relativity, he never considered that this would prevent his making evaluations and decried the view that said it would.

Fifth, Herskovitz emphatically distinguished between cultural relativity and concepts of the relativity of individual conduct. He considered the failure to make this distinction as the "most prominent among the confusions" when he responded to a major attack on cultural relativism.[14] He was certain that there must be conformity of the individual to the "code of the group" if there is to be "any regularity in life."[15] People must be enculturated into the groups in which they live, and they must adhere to their cultures. Cultural relativity, to

Herskovitz, could never mean that each individual does whatever he or she wished. He wrote:

> The denial of validity to standards of conduct operating within a society would not only bring on moral, but perceptual anarchy, and social life would grind to a halt.[16]

Cultural relativity, as advanced by social scientists, does not destroy the possibility of knowledge but offers a broader, more inclusive, base for knowledge. For example, studying the families of one community provides insights, but utilizing similar studies from various cultures gives us a far better potential for reaching deeper understanding. What cultural relativity often does is destroy certain parochial, limited ideas. It may compel us to see the world differently.

The fear of Christian absolutists is that their own faith will be considered to be parochial and, as a consequence, will be jettisoned by those who are persuaded to accept cultural relativity. The prevailing views of social science confirm their fear. Unfortunately, assertions and attacks by absolutists reinforce the view that limits the alternatives to only absolutism and faith or relativism and unbelief.

Examples for Understanding the Concept

Albert Einstein is remembered for his work in proposing and establishing the mathematical theory of relativity. It was a very different type of relativity, of course, but in trying to provide a simplified explanation of his theory, he used the following idea, one that is helpful in thinking about cultural relativity: a person traveling on a railroad walks forward in the train. Perhaps the person has walked, in terms of measured steps, thirty yards, yet in terms of location of his body in geographical space, he has moved four miles because of the movement of the train. How far has he walked? How far has he ridden? Einstein's point was that a simple statement of distance measuring change of location does not accurately answer the question. An answer must also include the context in which the change of location occurred.[17]

An idea, also, must always be placed in a context. If, as is usually true in everyday life, people communicate within their own cultural setting, then understanding will be reasonably well-attained. When people communicate from different social contexts, however, understanding is always limited, unless at least some participants understand the differences in social contexts. Consider the following example: being nice is valued when it is considered appropriate, but what is or is not nice is difficult to judge outside of the social context in which it occurs. In other words, one cannot define what is nice without taking into account the culture itself. Behavior that is defined as nice in one cultural context will not be seen as such in another. In the statements that follow, first an American, then a Costa Rican, describe the custom of teasing in Costa Rica:

Bill: The people of this nation are cruel to handicapped persons. In my year here, I've seen grown men teasing a mentally retarded boy. I've seen boys pitching pebbles at an old man who'd rage at them; I've heard people whistling and jeering at homosexuals. Even in private homes, I've seen grandparents teased. To top it off last week at the migration office, a lad went to a window and asked what time the office would close. A bad speech impediment forced him to use "l" instead of "r." The government clerk responded loudly, mocking the impediment by using an "l" for each "r" in her answer. The office staff laughed.

Carlos Valenciano: Bill sees and hears teasing, but he misunderstands it. To be teased is to be a part of the family. We keep handicapped people in our homes and treat them like anyone else. Sure, we tease them in anyway we can. In the United States, you put handicapped and elderly people away in institutions where you don't talk at all with them. That is what I would call cruelty.[18]

Herskovitz cited an example of how a perception of a straight line that seems so natural to us was so difficult for a person whose perceptions were from a culture of curved lines:

An example of how the enculturative experience shapes perception may be drawn from the West African country of Ghana. An electrical contractor was explaining a problem with which he was constantly confronted. "When a trench for a conduit must be dug, I run a line between the two points, and tell my workers to follow it. But at the end of the job, I invariably find that the trench has curves in it." The answer was simple, when sought in terms of the culturally influenced patterns of perception of his workers. For these were men from the northern part of the country, where circular forms predominate and where the straight line plays a minor role. They do not live in what has been called a carpentered world, so that to follow a straight line marked by a cord is as difficult for them as it would be for those of us whose learning experience stresses the perception and allocation in space of rectangular forms to describe, freehand, a perfect circle.[19]

Charles H. Kraft wrote about his first experience as a Christian missionary in northern Nigeria. One of the first questions he was asked by the Nigerians was, "Do you believe in evil spirits?" He realized that he did not know the answer because American culture "denies the reality of evil spirits."[20] Later, when he asked church leaders what their biggest problem was, they replied that it was a continuing difficulty with evil spirits. It was at this point that he began to recognize that there were many statements in the Bible that made reference to this type of problem. He further realized, "From my cultural perspective I had virtually ignored these passages, since they scratched me where I didn't itch."[21] Another example that Kraft cites concerns differences in meaning derived from differences in culture:

Dr. Jacob Loewen once asked a group made up of Africans and missionaries to tell him the main point of the story of Joseph in the Old Testament. The European missionaries all pointed to Joseph as a man who remained faithful to God no matter what happened to him. The Africans, on the other hand, pointed to Joseph as a man, who, no matter how far he traveled, never forgot his family. Both of these meanings are legitimate understandings of the passage. But differing cultural backgrounds led one group to one interpretation and the other group to the other interpretation.[22]

These illustrations of the relationship of meaning to the cultural context provide a basis of empirical evidence for cultural relativity. Every situation that brings together people from diverse cultural backgrounds can provide, for those who are sensitive to the situation, numerous evidences of cultural relativity. The work of anthropologists and sociologists has documented this repeatedly. In whatever way people interact in cultures distinct from their own, they have experiences that point to this basic social process that social scientists conceptualize as relativity. It is possible, of course, to interact cross-culturally without perceiving relativity. In such situations, people inevitably evaluate the other culture from an ethnocentric viewpoint and make their judgments. Usually they do not understand the situations in which they find themselves. Yet there are others who have never studied the subject, but who, by their sensitivity, can develop a good understanding of the relativity of culture.

The Status of Cultural Relativism in Social Science

In 1939 Clyde Kluckhohn expressed a widely accepted view among anthropologists when he described cultural relativism as "probably the most meaningful contribution which anthropological studies have made to general knowledge."[23] In his 1984 address to the American Anthropological Association, Clifford Geertz stated that there exists no need to defend relativism because it is "merely there, like Transylvania."[24] This did not mean, however, that there was no controversy about the theory. The theory has had a "curiously chequered career because of continuing disagreements among social scientists."[25] Hatch's book, for example, developed the theme that cultural relativism has been increasingly abandoned over the last thirty-five years.[26]

What has happened? Many things have occurred, but they do not justify Hatch's negative assessment. One evident factor was identified by Geertz: "It is by way of the idea of relativism, grandly ill-defined that [anthropology] has most disturbed the general intellectual peace."[27]

And it is not just the Christian publications that are disturbed. Paul Johnson's already cited book, *Modern Times,* sees relativity as the source of the problems of the contemporary age. David Glover concludes that relativity raises the problem of knowledge "in such an acute form that the possibility of saving rationality is in doubt."[28] William Shepherd has written that "all versions of relativism can [now] be critically detonated."[29] These are examples of what Geertz sees as the "dread of relativism" that results in an anti-relativism that he has perceived to be "broadly on the rise."[30]

Geertz also pointed out that it was not anthropological theory that led to the acceptance of relativism—it was anthropological data.[31] But the attacks do not grow out of data. Johnson made his sweeping conclusions of historical events without reference to data on human behavior. Shepherd's attack was based upon sociobiology—a field of study with a comprehensive theory of human behavior but no data on human subjects. He postulated that there is a "pancultural religion" drawn from the "long time scale" of biological evolution.[32] But he cited no data.

A second factor that gives rise to attacks upon cultural relativism is the view that the concept itself is relative. Therefore, as culture changes, the understanding of cultural relativity also changes. But relativists do not deny this. To expect it to be an impermeable absolute is to deny the insight that the theory itself proposes. Hatch's interpretation is interesting. He sees both World War II and the postwar period as altering the perceptions of cultural relativity. World War II was, he believes, a "moral embarrassment to ethical relativism."[33] He stated that "a woman who had lost a son in the war effort was not likely to grant that Hitler's culture was as valid as her own."[34] That is understandable. But it presupposes that cultural relativism prohibits the making of cross-cultural evaluations. This view is not prevalent among relativists and, as has already been discussed, is in no sense a necessary part of relativism. Advocates of cultural relativism should expect that, over time, the understanding of relativism and its use will change.

Hatch's point is important in identifying a third reason for the questioning of relativism: as time passes, social science moves on to new questions about which it gathers data. As it does this, it should reexamine old points of view in light of new data.

The Second World War did produce a sense of moral clarity. The outrages of the Nazis seem to clearly justify a consensus about the war. According to Hatch, it set into motion "sentiment that it may be possible after all to arrive at a set of ultimate values, such as those of freedom and humanity." The optimism following the war created a sense that "modern society may not be so absurd after all."[35] The possibility of international communication through the United Nations and other structures seemed to suggest the possibility that cross-cultural conflict could be overcome. The search for common values turned attention away from the fascination with diversity. Anthropology also sought to pursue these interests. It turned its interest toward "achieving scientific regularities" and "broad theory" in the study of culture.[36] Hanson's interpretation was that attention turned from an emphasis on cultural differences to "cultural similarities and human universals." He has also stated that the increasing interest in applied anthropology turned the attention of many away from issues of relativity toward the application of analyses within single cultural setting.[37]

But these changing interests did not mean the abandonment of cultural relativity. Kaufman wrote in 1960 that though there were many controversies, there was also a tendency among writers to "take for granted that relativity . . . is a demonstrated fact."[38] Fifteen years later, Hanson noted that anthropologists had written almost nothing about the subject in their journals during the 1960s. Yet, in the teaching of anthropology, cultural relativism remained prominent, accepted, and important.[39] Even though research interest had turned to other issues, cultural relativity was an important component of anthropology. Hanson predicted a revival of research interest in "this important concept."[40]

A fourth factor should also be noted. Controversy is a necessary part of the work of science. An idea as basic and imporant as relativism should be regularly reexamined, even though it has been established for many years. It may need to be revised or abandoned when new data results in new theory.

The current status of cultural relativism is that it is under attack by some, yet it remains as an accepted part of the social scientific position. The attacks upon it have not been based upon data. The fieldwork data that supports cultural relativism continues to confirm it. In spite of ongoing controversies, it is accurate to represent cultural relativity as a basic component of the social sciences. It is considered to be an operating theory based upon empirical evidence that is useful in understanding human behavior. We have every reason to try to understand it and can reasonably expect that its impact will continue in the forseeable future. Whatever controversies it may generate, the data of cross-cultural experience suggests that it will continue to be an important component of the social sciences and the New Class segment of our society.

5

Relativity in Context

What is truth on one side of the Pyrenees is error on the other.
—Blaise Pascal

The understanding of relativism can be enhanced by including four issues that involve the context in which real people live in the real world. The first is the fact of pluralism. The second is the relativizing effect that pluralism has for knowledge. The third is that in spite of relativism, it is still important to people to be part of a culture. And the fourth topic is the nature of the relationship between social science and society itself. These four topics provide a context within which to consider the case of relativism.

The Role of Pluralism

To encounter a culture different from one's own is to be in a situation that raises in some form the issues of relativity. Since most people in most times have lived in relative isolation from other cultures, ethnocentric viewpoints have been easily maintained. Indeed, even in our supposedly cosmopolitan age, our own communication patterns probably are more homogeneous than we realize. The meaningful conversations that most people have are most likely with others of a similar social class, educational, ethnic, and even religious background. In such conversation our ideas are comparatively unchallenged. At those times when our communication is uninhibited, it is usually with those people who are closest to our own beliefs. Conversely, when we communicate with people from somewhat different cultures, "politeness" causes us to hold back some of our thoughts.

The study of culture by the early social scientists led them to realize not only the value in studying diverse cultures but also to recognize their own ethnocentrism. Christian missionaries, by the nature of their work, also encountered cultures which were different from their own. But their role differed in an essential characteristic: they were supposed to proselytize the people of the alien culture. They could not be the detached observers that the social scientists had made part of their role. This necessarily complicated the role of the missionaries. Understanding the culture was important for effectiveness, but their goal was conversion.

The missionary situation has also been different from that of the American pastor. For the American minister, ethnocentric statements are likely to do no damage, because he and the congregation share a culture. Being ethnocentric can, in fact, help the American pastor to be successful, as people often are very responsive to such appeals. But such ethnocentrism can render the missionary ineffective. While the missionary movement has often been criticized for its ethnocentrism, it is also a matter of record that within this movement much creative wrestling with pluralism and cross-cultural communication has occurred.[1]

In recent years increasing numbers of Americans back home have encountered a broader range of cultural diversity. The inherent pluralism of American society has become more widely recognized. Movements of minorities within cities and regions have brought people into more contact with others who are culturally different from themselves. Increased levels of education have been accompanied by an increased awareness of cultural diversity. Increased occupational mobility and affluence have produced more movement of people into places they otherwise would not have gone. The television age—augmented by satellite networks—has increased the awareness of images and events from around the world. When Americans watched on television the cremation of Indira Ghandi it was, for most, a startling exposure to pluralism.

It may be worthwhile to remind ourselves that it has only been a few decades since people had access to such images only by watching newsreels at local movie theatres. Only a short period earlier, photographs alone could provide images. And we are still little more than a century removed from the time when only an artist could produce an image of somewhere else. The import of all of this is to recognize that we live only a few generations after a time when people experienced a level of isolation and a lack of knowledge of pluralism that would astound us. Yet that is the way most people in most cultures have lived. We are bearing the brunt of the recent impact of pluralism. What it does to our thinking is not necessarily pleasant. As Peter Berger has noted, once we face the alternatives of competing ideas of truth, we must choose. And having done this, we cannot forget that we have chosen.[2] When people know the truth on both sides of the Pyrenees, society will never be the same.

A fashionable term recently coined refers to the world as a "global village." This image suggests that we can no longer live in ethnocentric isolation but must come to grips with pluralism and what it means. We must find some way to deal with the Disney-expressed fact that "it's a small world after all." The way to do this is not clear. It is tempting to assert the superiority of one's own culture over others. But it is also unlikely to work, because this simply generates hostility among others who similarly view the situation from their own cultural perspective.

The challenge imposed by pluralism to our ways of thinking was stated very well by Forell:

> Pluralism, the existence of various and contradictory approaches to life simultaneously, which can neither be uprooted nor overcome, absorbed or ignored, is the ideologically most threatening aspect of the modern world. It is so threatening because it undermines the notion of "one truth" and thus jeopardizes equally the claims of atheists and theists, nationalists and internationalists, totalitarians and democrats . . . It has wrought havoc with the homogeneity of world Communism . . . it has threatened the underlying assumptions of melting-pot America, and it has undermined the discussion of ethics, aesthetics, and epistemology.[3]

It is important to note that pluralism does not simply question Christian truth but all ideology. In doing so, it is at least as much an ally of the Christian as it is an enemy. As Forell noted, it challenges competing claims to truth as well as those of the Christian. People of different cultures who live near each other, or in some way meaningfully communicate, must live with the explicit realization that their own truth is not the only truth by which people live. While we all know there are alternative "truths" intellectually, their impact is limited unless we have more immediate contact with them. We all know there are Buddhists, but the impact would be different if we had a neighboring family who was Buddhist. There would be a still greater impact if we got together with the neighbors, liked them, and gained respect for their way of life. It would increase still more if we lived in a Buddhist land.

Pluralism always has the potential to raise the epistemological question; that is, the question of how we know what we know. Quite simply put, a youth raised in a community where every person was either active in some form of Christian religion, or at least gave basic assent to it, would display a different set of "knowing" than a youth raised in a village where a portion of the population was Muslim, a portion Buddhist, and a small group was Christian. The concepts of cultural relativism in such a situation no longer are a method of study but involve very basic and important questions as to the nature of knowledge—the questions of epistemology.

The Epistemological Question

Because pluralism challenges the idea of absolute truth, the question of how we know becomes important. It is usually an uncomfortable question to face. Most of us would find it irritating if someone regularly questioned statements we make by asking how we know what we have asserted is true. The irritation stems from the fact that our statements if scrutinized carefully are usually found to be based upon very little evidence. They are derived from cultural prescriptions that are passed along and "taken for granted." I do not know, for example, what fluoride does or does not do for teeth. I do not know that the moon causes the tides of the ocean. In fact, I know very little, but I pass along a great deal of information that is "general knowledge" and that I accept as true. How does a person know whether the Bible is God's revelation? Indeed, how does anyone know anything unless there is direct empirical experience? Even then there may be reason for doubt. If you thought you saw a ghost last night, you probably still do not believe in ghosts because you "know" there is no such thing. Charles Kraft, a Bible believer, found that he did not believe in evil spirits though he knew that the Bible made repeated reference to them.[4]

The exploration of the question of epistemology is beyond the scope of this book. Nevertheless, a short consideration may be helpful. In his book, *Invitation to Sociology,* Peter Berger provides an excellent short introduction to the question of epistemology from the standpoint of the sociology of knowledge: he states what the study of social processes has shown concerning how individuals develop what they believe to be true knowledge—the way in which they define reality. It is rooted in the situation where an individual expresses to another person his or her subjective experiences. If others have experiences that are relatively congruent, individuals will interpret this as evidence that their views are objectively real. As others communicate in terms that also are relatively congruent, there emerges the confident belief that it is a matter of truth.

For example, quite often an individual will be in a group and wonder if the temperature of the room is a little too warm. The feeling that the room is not comfortable is a subjective experience. Usually a glance at others will give an indication as to what they are experiencing. The person may, however, wish more information and ask if the room is too warm. The request is for specific information from others. If others also respond that it is unusually warm, a definition of reality is reached that the room is uncomfortably warm. If, however, the others say the room is quite pleasant, a different definition of reality is reached that is likely to be that the individual "may be coming down with something." There are, of course, other possibilities. Some people, over a period of time, come to expect that they prefer a cooler room than others and would interpret this discrepancy as normal. There are many combinations of interpretation. The crucial point is that it is by expressing our subjective experiences that we develop a definition of objective reality. When the definition is developed it is believed to be objective reality—that is, it is true apart from what one thinks about it.

We are not normally aware of this process. We are particularly not aware of it in those more abstract and complex matters that make up our beliefs and norms, compared to rather simple and measurable matters such as room temperature. The process, however, is the same. Our definitions are based upon the ongoing conversations we have with other people. "Subjective reality," Peter Berger has written, "hangs on the thin thread of conversation."[5]

When a matter is defined as real, it is accepted as true and can become a part of the "taken-for-granted" world. It may become internalized as part of the personality. Those matters that have been internalized are accepted as "of-course-that-is-true" propositions. Many of these may be accepted because of the authority of those who are thought to have stated them; our conversation has defined them as people who know and can be trusted. In this way I accept the influence of the moon upon the tides, though I have had no experience of it. It is part of my subjective experience that scientists say this is so, and a number of other persons have said that it is so, and there are no persons I consider to be credible who are saying anything contrary. Because of this I have confidently explained this "truth" to my children.

My subjective experience of any situation will be influenced not only by the event, but also by those cultural definitions that are familiar to me and that I have at least to some extent internalized. My experience of being a teacher or a father or whatever is not just a matter of the event but also that which culture teaches me will be involved. To be a woman today is thus very different from being a woman fifty years ago, because the cultural knowledge that tells a woman what to expect and what it means to be a woman is quite different.

Another influence on what is experienced is praxis. In this usage, praxis refers to the circumstances of any situation. Circumstances will always influence the subjective experience. The automobile age is different from all previous ages just because we now have "wheels." It has changed the range of options for shopping, for working, and for social interaction. As this range of options has changed, so has the nature of our experiences and thus the definitions of reality—the culture—have also changed.

That the culture that defines truth for people develops out of social processes does not mean that it is a mechanical process. People within a group have a variety of experiences that make them open to already defined truth in various ways. People within a group vary in their awareness of other cultures, which means varying awareness of alternative ways of doing things and alternative definitions of truth. The decisions that people make place them in different social contexts, resulting in their having different experiences as well as exposures to different conversations. When I chose a college to attend, I chose not only a college but a whole social setting. When assigned to a place to live (or when a place was chosen), I put myself into a specific context. The choice of a college was made on the basis of several factors. The choice put me in a social setting which had an impact far beyond anything that I could contemplate. There are many twists in the entangled processes by which our lives develop, even though they all involve the same basic processes of knowing.

The social process by which knowledge is defined provides a different concept from that which we usually hold. We conventionally tie knowledge directly to evidence. That is, if you produce the evidence I will accept the facts. Knowledge, as social scientists perceive it, is certainly not removed completely from evidence, but it is far more tied to social processes than to direct empirical evidence.

A common reaction to the analysis of the social process by which knowledge develops is that it reduces knowledge to being "just somebody's idea." Thus, if dating customs in our society define one set of behaviors while those in another culture define a different set, this may be then interpreted to mean that what one does is "just a matter of culture." By this expression, it is implied that there is no objective reality in the process apart from the ideas someone holds.

This view misses two essential points in understanding how we know. First, it has become a sociological axiom that "things that are defined as real are real in their consequences." The consequences of knowledge occur no matter what an individual's idea may be. For example, the idea that people of the black race are inferior to those of the white race and therefore were appropriately used as slaves was "just an idea." But it was shared among people who acted upon it. It led to a wide range of attitudes and behaviors both by those who accepted it and those who opposed it. It led to opportunities for some to be slaveholders and denied opportunities to others who were reduced to the existence of slaves. The termination of slavery unsettled the culture but led to the development of new ideas of what was true that were expressed in a system of segregation. Decades after such segregation has been ruled illegal, the results of the idea continue and influence not only thinking but behavior as well.

A tree is real in the sense that a person will bump into it whether one knows it is there. The cultural definition of race is there also whether one knows it is there. A person will "bump" into it even if the person knows nothing about it. Cultural reality is different from the natural reality of the tree. But it is not just "someone's idea." It is a form of objective reality by virtue of its having been socially defined. Cultural relativity does not deny that the definitions of a culture are real and that members need to participate in them. To ignore them is to ignore reality. It is a social reality, it is true, but in this it is still very real and has real consequences.

Secondly, the process by which knowledge develops does not in any way contradict the idea that there is ultimate truth. It does not suggest that one idea is as valid as any other. Neither does it suggest that anything could be considered true if a group decided it was true. Knowledge, in any group, is derived from the subjective experiences of the people within the group. Thus cultures vary in what they define as food, but no culture can define pebbles as food. Obviously, the subjective experience of the people would not sustain such an idea. Cultures have wide variations in beliefs and norms, but these are all rooted in the experiences of people.

The distinction between what is ultimately true and our knowledge of our world must always be distinguished. It is our knowledge that is a consequence of our social processes and thus relative to our culture. But because it is our own culture and grounded in our own experience, it seems to be self-evidently true. Pluralism calls this into question and originates the issue of relativity.

The Necessity of Being in a Culture

Accepting the relativity of culture does not free us from society. It is not a satisfactory resolution to simply stand apart. Every individual requires a meaningful set of social relationships if life is to be at all satisfactory. Physical health, mental health, and social well-being all relate statistically to interaction with others. The more isolated an individual, the more likely some form of illness will occur. To have meaningful social relationships, it is necessary to share in a culture that provides an interpretation of reality through beliefs and norms and provides for an orderly society in which to interact. It is not necessary for the individual to accept every cultural definition, but it is necessary to participate sufficiently so that one can interact meaningfully with others. People with no knowledge of sports have difficulty relating to sports fans precisely because they are unable to share their definitions and thus their enthusiasm. If one does not share cultural definitions, one cannot have meaningful ties, and the result is isolation. Conversely, belonging is a consequence of sharing the definitions and enthusiasm of the group. Sociologists, I admit, often fail to mention this aspect, though it can be deduced from the sociological literature.

Just as individuals are dependent upon culture, culture is dependent upon individuals. Culture exists only in the minds of those who share in it. If individuals do only whatever each thinks is right without any reference to a culture, in effect there is no culture. The ability of a culture to define reality and provide an orderly society in which people can live is dependent upon the acceptance of the culture by its members. If there are no beliefs and norms that define reality, there can be no order or viability. It is thus necessary for citizens to support the culture and the cultural definitions and to sanction those ideas and persons who would disrupt it. Indeed, in a very real sense, those who would disrupt the definitions provided by a culture endanger the very social order itself. There is a mutual interest, then, between the nature of the definitions of reality that are self-perpetuating and the interests of the individuals that the culture be strong and ongoing.

The implications of this human need to participate in a culture are crucial. If the culture fails to define beliefs and norms, the individuals experience meaninglessness. Similarly, an individual who refuses to participate in a culture will experience loneliness and meaninglessness. These findings seem to be rooted in the basic characteristics of humanness, just as is the relativity of the culture. Shakespeare's statement that "nothing [is] either good or bad but thinking makes it so" is not only wrong in the eyes of Christian absolutists; it is also wrong for the cultural relativists. It is wrong for the relativists, because culture is grounded in the experiences of people, participation in a culture is necessary, and such participation requires adhering to the cultural traits of that group. Furthermore, that group must develop norms and beliefs that benefit its functioning. It could not, for example, function well if it allowed its members to have possessions but also to steal possessions from each other at will. The resulting conflict would ultimately destroy the group. To say that culture is relative is not to say that "anything goes."

Social Science and Society in Conflict

The acknowledged conflicts between Christianity and social science must not prevent us from recognizing another conflict that is seldom mentioned—the incipient conflict between society and social science. It is, in fact, the same basic tension as that between social science and Christianity. The elements have already been discussed, but the issue can now be enjoined by reviewing and bringing them together.

Science is inherently critical. It seeks to see through the relationships of variables. It seeks to find out what causes what. Social science turns this critical eye towards society and its culture. Instead of trying to increase and preserve the cultural definition of reality, it tries to find out why certain cultural traits exist. In other words, sociology's approach is not "patriotic" in trying to interpret the society in the best possible light. Rather, it attempts to understand the society as it really is. It is in the very nature of sociology as a science that it seeks to take apart, analyze, and make explicit the very elements that the patriotism needs to promote its definition of reality and order. It is in this sense that Peter Berger refers to sociology as a subject which debunks the social systems it is studying.[6] It refuses to accept at face value the "public relations handouts" of society and insists on trying to fathom how the systems really work.

It is not inevitable that sociology will fulfill its critical function. It has often relinquished this function and provided its services as teacher and researcher to reinforce the social system. So also have other sciences. The social sciences in communist countries seem to have abdicated critical analyses, and their reports simply process statistics without any theoretical base. Peter Burke has noted that the priority so often given to history in the school curriculum is related to the needs of society to justify itself.

> Governments saw history as a means of promoting national unity, as education for citizenship, or, as a less sympathetic observer might have put it, as propaganda.[7]

It is not necessary to spend a great amount of time in the discussion of school issues before it becomes evident that many people in America expect the history course to provide support for just these purposes. Similarly, if economics is taught, it is expected to build support for the economic system of the society. Indeed, the critical function of social science is not appreciated by many who see it as destructive. And, from what I am contending here, such a view is essentially correct. The critical function of social science stands in opposition to the needs of society and its culture to bind together people into a common set of beliefs and norms.

It is not by chance that sociology developed in the western democracies of Germany, France, England, Canada, and the United States. Within these societies there is the belief that the critical function is necessary. That is, the critical role is seen as essential for the testing of beliefs and norms, and it is thought that such testing will ultimately provide for a better society and culture. The vested interests that are in control must answer rather than silence the critics. Therefore, the culture is always adjusting to its current situation, renewing its plausibility, and people regain confidence in the system: the society is strengthened.

But in open societies, appreciation for the critical function seems to be always tenuous. Those in positions of leadership are tempted to see criticism as destructive rather than constructive. At best, it is considered an obstacle to the efficiency of their leadership. At worst, a critic is seen as "an enemy of the people." And the critics are also tempted to see themselves as fulfilling some special, superior role. It is heady to sit on the sidelines and point out all of the errors of those who are performing the functions of operating the society. One can become a chronic critic, where the critical function becomes an end in itself.

Social science is dependent for financial and social support upon the very society it criticizes. Only a society that believes that self-criticism strengthens it can tolerate a functioning science of society. The need of society to increase acceptance of its cultural beliefs and norms and the needs of sociology to be a critic of society are potentially conflicting. They are reconciled only by the cultural belief in the value of criticism as a corrective and strengthening device. Though that belief is often questioned, it is a crucial cornerstone of what makes a free society free.

Christian absolutists have much in common with all other builders of the society. They also are in the business of building groups that define reality in common through a set of beliefs and norms. They also find the criticisms of social science to be an obstacle, and they are correct in this. They are also correct to sense its potential for destructiveness. But this does not mean that its destructiveness is necessary. It may render benefits for Christianity even as it can for society.

6

The Absolutist Case against Cultural Relativity

> All the common definitions of relativism are framed by opponents
> of relativism . . . they are absolutist definitions.
>
> —John Ladd

Christian absolutists leave no doubt about their opposition to cultural relativity and their objections should be carefully weighed. There is a unanimity in the opposition, and Stephen Grunlan's statement of five major objections typifies well the absolutist case.[1]

1. "CULTURAL RELATIVITY LEADS TO ETHICAL RELATIVITY . . . [IT] SEEMS TO LEAVE US WITHOUT A BASIS FOR HUMAN MORALITY."[2]

This is the major criticism and is found in practically every absolutist critique of cultural relativity. It is an argument based on consequence: it does not examine whether the data supporting cultural relativism is accurate, but instead it is critical because of the perceived consequences of relativism. If our desire is to determine truth, we cannot discard an idea simply because the consequences are undesirable. As Kaufman has written, "If relativistic thinking seems to conflict with the logic and epistemology which previous generations, oriented toward absolutistic thought, have developed, this is no real argument against it."[3]

But this objection does deserve to be evaluated sympathetically. To destroy the basis of morality would be, without question, a most serious consequence. For the absolutist who is convinced that relativity has destroyed morality, it is very difficult even to consider the possibility that knowledge could be relativistic. For individuals whose faith is built upon the idea that biblical revelation is absolute, relativism must be considered pernicious. This is a normal and expected reaction. Conversely, for those who do not believe the Bible to be absolute, the acceptance of relativity would not pose this difficulty. The issue needs better exploration than the name-calling often resorted to where relativists are considered to be destructive or absolutists are thought to be dangerously narrow-minded.

Does cultural relativity leave society without a basis for morality? A survey of cultures makes it evident that there are functioning systems of morality in societies that have had no contact with Judaic or Christian religion. There are also people within our culture who do not accept the authority of the Bible or of any Christian revelation but who have internalized a moral code. Anthropological literature confirms that most of the cultures of the world have been non-Christian yet have contained functioning codes of morality.

These cultures, however, usually considered their own morality to be absolute. The important question remains: Can a society that is relativistic have a functioning moral code? Absolutists assert confidently that it could not. Paul Johnson has stated that the turmoil of the twentieth century, including the atrocities of Hitler, were a result of moral relativism.[4] (Earlier, I noted that Bronowski attributed Hitler's atrocities to absolutism.)

Tim LaHaye has concluded that "most of the evils in the world today can be traced to humanism."[5] He further states that the "elimination of absolutes always produces chaos, followed by repression."[6] Carl F. H. Henry has contended that without "transcendentally revealed truth . . . [there is] no logical option but to concede that rape, terrorism and murder may be as right as their opposites, or that the value of a camel may be as great as that of a man."[7] This last charge sounds terrifying, but does it make any sense? For example, who has claimed that rape is as right as its opposite? (What is its opposite?) Is not the terrorism of postrevolutionary Iran the work of absolutists? Indeed, terrorism is often the consequence of absolutism. Who claims that a camel is as great as a man?

In spite of such overstatements, a deep concern is evident in Henry's charges. In his view, relativists will consider themselves to be beyond any specific moral principle at any particular time. Unbound by moral codes, they will act without restraint and will, indeed, feel justified in encouraging others to do the same. Is there evidence of this?

Unfortunately, there is no way to test this question. The sources of behavior are always complex and intertwined. While it is undeniable that there are tremendous problems in the world, they cannot necessarily be traced to cultural relativism. Relativists may not have great virtue, but it is difficult to find evidence of undue vice either. What absolutists seem to ignore is the role of absolutists in all manner of crimes against people. Any reader of history finds examples such as those in the *Fox's Book of Martyrs* that demonstrate that being an absolutist—including a Christian absolutist—is no guarantee that one will not lie, cheat, steal, or kill. In earlier ages when the Christian religion controlled kingdoms and absolutes were secure there were repeated horrors of criminality, senseless warfare, persecution, and repression. And this is not a uniquely Catholic failure; the record of Protestantism has its own examples. Indeed, history provides numerous reasons for relativists to fear Christian absolutists.

The records of history are littered with sufficient acts of cruelty that we can find evidence to support any thesis by selecting the focus. The historical record of some Christian absolutists is not one in which to take comfort. It is undeniable that there have been individuals who have considered themselves above the law and thus able to perpetrate crimes. That relativity produces people of vice with greater frequency and intensity than absolutism has been charged but not proven. It is, however, probable that we cannot successfully counter relativism simply by contending that it is not good for us. The empirical evidence that it is an accurate model of human knowledge is too conclusive. Its power lies not in the fact that it is being taught in a classroom but in the experiences people have with pluralism.

But there is another consideration which is of overriding importance for our purpose: the basis of morality as presented in the Bible. Genesis portrays the understanding that God created a woman because it was "not good for the man to be alone."[8] But the loneliness could only be overcome if there was some mutual sharing and understanding. Any relationship between people is inevitably moralistic. That is, the existence of meaning among people creates a definition of what is appropriate and necessary behavior among them in their relatedness. People who are married, work together, or share any activity over time develop expectations of each other that define and compel certain behaviors. In this sense morality is inevitable. The ideas of fact and the ideas of morality that are the components of culture are not superfluous but necessary for the relatedness of human beings. The moral code is thus grounded in the basic needs of the individual. They arise in every culture because they are a necessity for human existence and are rooted in human experience. They are equally necessary whether one is a cultural relativist or a Christian absolutist. This relationship between loneliness, morality, and culture is a biblical principle and consistent with social science.

As I have already noted in the fourth chapter, Melvin Herskovitz found the idea that relativism destroyed morality particularly misguided. His position was that the basis for human morality was still right where it had always been—in the culture. Further, he pointed out, the individual must participate in the culture, must be socialized into it, and must internalize most of its beliefs and norms. To do otherwise is destructive to the individual as well as the society.

It is possible that social science has in some way contributed to the rampant individualism of our own culture. But this must not obscure the larger factors at work. There is a great need for more research into the processes by which cultural ties develop. Indeed, the understanding of human behavior that has developed within the social sciences provides a foundation for the study of the strengthening of social ties and the reduction of anomie. Such application is needed. Whatever influence social science may have had for the good or ill of society, it can not destroy the basis for morality that is identified by both biblical teaching and sociological perspective. That basis—grounded in the human need for relationship—is universal.

The first criticism is not based upon evidence but consequence. But even though dreadful consequences are considered sure by some, the evidence is not conclusive. The criticism is misguided, however, because the basis of human morality is found in human need.

2. "CULTURAL RELATIVITY IS ITSELF AN ABSOLUTE AND THEREFORE A CONTRADIC-
TION IN TERMS."[9]

This same charge has also been of concern to social scientists.[10] It may be persuasive in terms of logic. In terms of insight, however, it is not helpful. Concepts are, after all, mental symbols by which we try to understand reality. There are logical contradictions which help us to apprehend truth more clearly. These may be illustrated by paradoxes which Jesus frequently used: for example, he praised the peacemaker[11] but denied that he had come to bring peace insisting, instead, that he had come to bring a sword.[12] It may not be logically consistent to make both claims, but together as paradox they provide us with a better understanding of his approach.

Bertrand Russell, the atheist-mathematician-scientist, used to take great delight in finding logical contradictions that he thought clever, and that he considered to have settled the question:

> If everything must have a cause, then God must have a cause. If there can be anything without a cause, it may just as well be the world as God, so that there cannot be any validity in that argument. It is exactly of the same nature as the Hindu's view, that the world rested upon an elephant and the elephant rested upon a tortoise; and when they said, "How about the tortoise?" the Indian said, "Suppose we change the subject."[13]

Russell's argument is logical. Perhaps for some it was persuasive. It failed to have any significant impact, because it did not provide any useful insight or reflection on the understanding of reality. This is not to discredit logic nor to encourage the idea that it is irrelevant. The charge of a lack of logic is an important charge, and if it is found to be true, it must be carefully considered. But the discovery of what seems to be a logical contradiction is not in itself a conclusive argument.

But what then of the contradiction? The basis for cultural relativity is the empirical experience of the study of culture. If this is the finding and if it is accurate, it makes sense to say that cultural relativity can be a useful insight in understanding human behavior in various cultures. This is simply reporting a finding. It is a universal characteristic of human behavior, just as is the need of humans for relationships with others. To conclude that cultural relativity is a useful concept in understanding cultures is not to assert that cultural relativity is absolute. Indeed, it is not an absolute. It is currently a concept that has been found to provide insights into the processes of knowledge in cultures. As time passes, it will undoubtedly be revised and perhaps discarded. It is clearly a consequence of the cultural processes of social science and relative to that. But it also seems to provide the best basis, at this time, for understanding both processes of cultural knowledge and the comparison of that knowledge across cultures. Kaufman described his work as a relativist in these words:

> We know, of course, that our work in turn will be judged and rein-terpreted and changed by the work of others in the future, and we have no way of knowing what directions these reinterpretations will take; but we also know that this is the work which we who are living in this present have to do, and we know that we must do it in terms of the norms which have been given to us. . . . Hence, when one claims to be seeing the other finite positions in the history of thought as relative and limited, one is not really presupposing any claim to be transcending one's own finite position, or even the finite positions of the past, in an absolute fashion. One is merely claiming to be living in a creative present, from which the past can be understood in its limited character and which itself will be incorporated into that past by some future present.[14]

3. "CULTURAL RELATIVITY IS SELF-CONTRADICTORY . . . [IT] IMPLIES THAT ALL VALUES ARE CULTURAL AND THEREFORE RELATIVE. YET . . . [IT] STATES THAT ALL CULTURES ARE EQUALLY GOOD AND SHOULD BE RESPECTED EQUALLY."[15]

This objection expresses the idea that relativism will render us unable to make evaluations. But this is not at all a necessary deduction. In practice, cultural relativists believe their view to be an important antidote to ethnocentrism. That is why the cultural relativist insists that to understand another culture we must suspend judgment. But this does not mean that the suspension of judgment continues forever. Indeed, a basic benefit in the study of comparative cultures is to make evaluative comparisons. One of the most important early books that did much to create awareness of the need for a relativistic approach in the study of culture was Ruth Benedict's *Patterns of Culture.* In it she described three cultures and tried to demonstrate the need for the suspension of ethnocentrism in understanding these peoples. The reader of her book cannot help but be aware that Ms. Benedict preferred the Hopi over the Kwakiutl culture. She made her preference explicit. But in her work she also attempted to utilize cultural relativity as a guiding principle.

There have been some social scientists who have stated that all cultures are equally good, but theirs is very much a minority view.[16] That cultural relativists emphasize the importance of respect for each culture does not mean that evaluations of cultures cannot be made. The concern is for fairness and caution in making these judgments, acknowledging how easily an unrecognized ethno-centrism can distort understanding.

Hatch criticized Benedict's work for not displaying the tolerance of the relativists because she does make evaluations.[17] He missed the point of the quotation he had himself made from Herskovitz: "The relativist point of view brings into relief the validity of every set of norms for the people whose lives are guided by them."[18] Cultural relativity does assert that the norms are valid for those who hold them. But this only says the obvious: people believe what they believe. Anthropologists stress the need to accept beliefs sympathetically for the purpose of accurate understanding. Once understanding is gained, the anthropologist may make comparisons across cultures, making explicit the criteria used for evaluation in the comparisons. That is, in fact, a most important reason for undertaking such studies.

The bases upon which cultures are compared are also inevitably relative. If dictatorial governments make "the trains run on time," the standard of punctuality could be a basis for cross-cultural comparison. It is probably not the basis most of us would use. We would prefer the standard of freedom of thought and expression. It is common for Americans to evaluate nations on the basis of gross national product but not family solidarity. Inevitably, the standards are relative. It should not be surprising that the standards for comparison usually implemented by social scientists are different from those used by Christians. The relativist does insist that we should respect every culture in order to understand it. The relativist does not, however, prohibit evaluations.

4. "THE CONCEPT ITSELF IS ETHNOCENTRIC. THE CONCEPT IS A WESTERN IDEA AND REFLECTS A WESTERN BIAS. A THING IS GOOD IF IT IS FUNCTIONAL OR EFFICIENT."[19]

It is true that cultural relativity is a Western idea. More specifically, it is a concept of social science, and it has gained its meaning within a specific set of cultural traits. Its meaning is understood and shared within the community of social science. Its meaning must be understood within that context if it is to be understood accurately. It is itself, as has been noted, relative. This is all true, but these are not meaningful objections.

To contend that relativity is ethnocentric is to say that it distorts the work of the social scientist. Undoubtedly, social scientific work has sometimes distorted reality. Ethnocentrism is always a danger, and the social scientist is as subject to it as is anyone else. There are sufficient examples of social scientists being ethnocentric to establish such failings. But the concept itself is not necessarily ethnocentric.

The crucial question is, in what sense is this concept distorting or misrepresenting reality? It is quite likely that Professor Grunlan has found the whole impact of cultural relativity to be a distortion, and therefore felt that no citation of distortion was needed. Yet, in contending that the concept is inevitably a product of the culture, Grunlan is inadvertently supporting the idea that concepts are relative to their social context. It would be helpful if he had cited some evidence of distortion. That social science is subject to ethnocentrism does not constitute evidence that contradicts the empirical work of the anthropologists.

5. "CULTURAL RELATIVITY HAS LITTLE VALUE IN RESOLVING CROSS-CULTURAL CONFLICT."[20]

This is a difficult accusation to understand. Edward T. Hall's work has demonstrated that people from one culture often become involved in disputes simply because they attach a different meaning to time in keeping appointments. What one culture defines as a proper arrival time, another defines as being insultingly tardy. Cultural differences create conflict when people are not sensitive to the relativity of the beliefs and norms of other peoples. Cultural relativity indeed is a basic starting point for resolving such conflict.

It is true that the absolutist has a standard by which to resolve disputes. That standard is simply to insist upon the correctness of the absolutist's own point of view. It is not true, however, that this will help to resolve cross-cultural conflict. The other culture will be unlikely to accept the absolutists' standard.

The understanding gained from cultural relativity is perceived by social scientists to be invaluable in resolving cross-cultural disputes. However, whether cultural relativity contributes to resolving cross-cultural conflict is irrelevant to the validity of the concept. It may be valid and useful without helping to resolve cross-cultural conflict. Its value is an important matter but does not determine whether it is true.

In conclusion, the arguments used by absolutists against cultural relativism, no matter how sincere they may be, are not based upon data nor are they well-grounded. Although there may be relativists whose views are as the absolutists charge them to be, the considerations absolutists attack are neither necessary nor integral to the relativist position.

It is important to note that absolutists do not consider the evidence available for cultural relativity. By ignoring its basis and charging it with producing bad consequences, the issue of truth is ignored. Grunlan's opposition to relativity, for example, that it has bad consequences (destroys morality and does not resolve conflicts), bad characteristics (it is an absolute and ethnocentric), and inconsistency (it is self-contradictory) ignores the basic issue. What is not addressed is the issue of whether it is true. This would seem to be the basic point for evaluation of the concept.

In the next chapter we will turn to an additional and very different reason concerning why the objections to cultural relativity may prove to be comparatively unimportant. If the Bible reflects the absolutist point of view, the believing Christian would have reason to contend for that position. But what if the Bible's approach is relativistic? As improbable as that may seem to many, it should not be rejected without being examined. If this is the case, Christians would not need to attack relativism. What emerges is a case for Christian relativism—a view that utilizes the empirical work of social science, and that is fully consistent with the biblical text as interpreted by fundamentalist Christians.

A Consideration of Terms: Absolutes, Universals, and the Supracultural

Before considering the biblical text, a digression may be helpful in considering the absolutist situation. It is understandable that people believe their basic cultural values to be not only superior to those of others but to represent absolute truth. When we have internalized what our culture defines as true, our beliefs seem factual and self-evident. It is difficult to imagine that right thinking people could believe otherwise. Thus the belief that one's truth is absolute is a logical extension of those beliefs. This propensity is true for all beliefs, not just those held by Christians.

The existence of absolutes usually seems so simple. That one should not kill certainly must be an absolute. Yet, is there any society that accepts this as an absolute? Does not every society prescribe that there are specified times when certain people are required to kill certain other people? So when war is declared (the right time), soldiers are drafted (the right people to kill) and directed to attempt to engage and kill the enemy (the right people to be killed). But the meaning of all of these acts, as well as the norms, are tied up in the particular culture. If we were to continue to pursue this example, we would find that our attempts to specify an absolute position concerning killing would be most difficult. The more we attempt to be precise, the more difficult it is to say anything except that every behavior must be understood in its context. To specify a cross-cultural absolute proves to be amazingly difficult.

Some Christians have accepted the cultural relativism of human knowledge while making the distinction that God's message is absolute. Charles H. Kraft, in *Christianity in Culture*, concludes that all propositions about Christianity must be understood in their context. Human culture is inexorably relative.[21] He adds to this the assertion that God's truth is supracultural—it is above and outside culture.[22] He cites Eugene Nida that in Christianity there are absolutes that are supracultural truths, but these are all related to God and not to human understanding.[23]

Kraft contends that there are five reasons why these supracultural truths about God cannot be understood in their absolute character by humans:

> 1. The limitations of the revelations. God has seen fit to reveal only certain things concerning himself, his plans, and his purposes. That which he has not yet revealed we cannot know.
> 2. Our finiteness. We are limited in our understanding of even that which has been revealed . . .
> 3. Our sinfulness. Our perception and ability to understand and respond to God's revelation is, like every other aspect of our lives, affected at every point by sin. For this reason our motives are never completely pure nor our vision completely lucid.
> 4. Our cultural conditioning. The fact that we are totally immersed in a given culture conditions us to perceive of all reality, including God's revelation, in terms of that culture.
> 5. Our individual psychological and experiential conditioning. Even within shared cultural boundaries, the life experience of every individual is unique. This likewise conditions one's perception of the revelation.[24]

These five reasons that truths, as understood by humans, cannot be absolute are important and well-stated. But what do Kraft and Nida mean in adding that

God's message is a supracultural absolute? If it means that God is above and separate from culture, there is no problem. By definition, God is other than human. But if this is what is meant, the idea of the supracultural does not add anything to our understanding. It is a synonym for what has already been identified by another name.

And what does it mean to say that there are absolutes that are God's truths, but humans can know them only in a relative sense? Because we are all humans, the only concepts we have are held in human words. Therefore, all truths that we can know are relative, including what we know in Christianity. If God exists, is an absolute, and has revealed himself; that revelation, in its use of words, is using symbols that are human products and relative in meaning to the social context. The Bible was written in human words and has been understood and discussed by every generation in human language. If all human knowledge is cultural, then knowledge gained from the Bible is, in this sense, also cultural. The idea of the supracultural adds nothing to our understanding of how we know. Indeed, these writers are making a good case for relativity.

For social scientists the term "universal" is useful. In the preceding chapter it was stated that the human need for morality was found in all cultures and thus is a universal characteristic. Does that make this need absolute? The idea that traits may be universal refers to the fact that some characteristics are found in all cultures. Cultures vary greatly, but they also have much in common. To repeat an illustration used earlier, the definition of what is and is not food varies tremendously. However, a society cannot define any item it might choose and designate it as food. Food will be defined from among a range of items that provide at least some nutrition and acceptable taste. The common need for food is a universal trait for humans. The particular definition of food in a culture is relative to the culture. There are no food absolutes because of the variation in definitions. But because food is found in all cultures, it is referred to as a universal. Those traits which have been found to be universal are more general in nature. Specific definitions of behavior—what is usually meant by "absolutes"—have not been found. For example, families have been found to be universal in that in all cultures people live in family-like groupings. But because of the wide variation in specific definitions of family and in behaviors expected, social scientists have found no absolutes.

A culture must define beliefs and norms so that each human has an opportunity to sleep, eat, and eliminate. Certain specific traits will be clustered around the beliefs or norms so as to define these behaviors. They are relative to the culture and attempt to provide for the universal needs of the individuals. So also there is a universal need for meaningful interaction with others. There is a need for social order. In fact, many of the teachings that are considered a basic part of religion are simply the rules of order necessary for any social group to continue. "Thou shalt not steal." "Honor thy father and thy mother." These are basically the way a culture arranges for the social order; this order is a universal need.

It has been common among scholars to note the similarity among the major

religions of the world concerning teachings on social order. They have concluded—though I believe mistakenly—that because of this similarity, the world's
religions are essentially alike. In fact, all social codes are in some ways similar in
the prescriptions they contain for social order. But the religions of the world are
also very different in important ways. To say that Buddhism and Christianity are
basically similar because both prohibit theft overlooks vast differences in their
interpretations of the world and a person's role in it.

The prescriptions for social order relating to universal needs are important.
Every society must have a way of defining such matters as property ownership
and behavior. It is done differently in one society compared to another, but it is
always done. McGehee was stimulated by reading C. S. Lewis to develop a list of
such types of codes:

> Generally they are concerned with the principle of denial of self-interest
> in favor of the interests of others. They also are concerned with the idea of
> personal responsibility vis-à-vis others and the right of others to expect
> reasonable behavior from individuals which is not self-serving. At the same
> time they involve an understanding and acceptance of inherent weaknesses
> in humans. In short, they involve such concepts as courtesy, respect,
> consideration, honesty, integrity, loyalty, fidelity, charity, duty, respon-
> sibility, accountability, appropriateness, and desert, to name a few. They
> are reflected in codes of conduct throughout history and are the heart of
> what Lewis describes as "the Tao."[25]

The items McGehee lists are necessary traits for strengthening and reinforcing
a culture. Yet, American society in recent years has pursued a rampant individualism and has given little attention to them. In an earlier era they were given
much attention. Is it not a likely hypothesis that it is this individualism and lack
of social ties that has had far more destructive impact on society than has
relativism? The fear of some absolutists that ideas of cultural relativity will
undermine the culture fails to recognize what social scientists have increasingly
realized—that culture requires order and meaning, or it fails the needs of its
members. A recognition of the reality of cultural relativity in no way changes
these universal requirements of culture.

Some Conclusions

The case against cultural relativism seems to be based on a prior commitment
to an absolutist position and a fear of the consequences of relativism. This is
understandable. It is also understandable that some absolutists utilize extreme
statements of relativists and exaggerate the relativist position. The mutual
isolation between Christian absolutists and relativists also tends to perpetuate
the lack of understanding.

Yet, humans must have culture, social order, and morality. There is no escape from these, though they are often violated. The major question for all humans who perceive alternatives is this: by which culture, order, and morality will we live?

No matter how well-intentioned the absolutist attack on relativity may be, this attack needs to be examined from another perspective. Absolutists assume that their position is based upon biblical principles and the attack is necessary to defend biblical truth. What if they are mistaken?

Part III
Biblical Religion

7

Relativity and Biblical Religion

Abraham is our father.
—John 8:39

Both relativists and absolutists believe biblical religion is absolutist. And both think cultural relativity is incompatable with absolutism. To relativists, the absolutism of the Bible is a reason to regard it as inadequate for the contemporary mind. To absolutists, the Bible is God's message, and its teachings must be absolute. What has been ignored by both sides is the question as to whether biblical religion actually is absolutist. If the Bible should be found not to be absolutist, then a reconsideration by both positions would be in order. Sometimes such simple, basic assumptions remain unexamined.

There are certainly biblical passages that have been used to support absolutist interpretations. Probably the one most often cited has contained Jesus' words: "I am the way, the truth, and the life; no one comes to the Father, but by me."[1] The apostles also made similar statements. The words of Peter seem to support this interpretation: "There is salvation in no one else, for there is no other name under heaven given among men by which we must be saved."[2]

Because of the emphasis given to such texts, contemporary Christians are understandably confident in their assertions that Christianity is absolutist. Whatever our contemporary ideas about the relativism of culture, the origins of the Christian faith seem clearly to have been absolutist. The claims for this seem justified. Thus Tim LaHaye writes, "The Judeo-Christian ethic . . . [is] absolute—not subject to revision or deletion by any earthly potentate or Supreme Court."[3] Grunlan adds, "Christians claim a universal moral standard in the Word of God."[4]

In spite of this, Christians who are informed and sensitive about the role of culture cannot ignore the evidence of its influence on the social process of knowledge. So David Lyon, a Christian sociologist, has written:

> Knowledge is ever produced in the context of cultural belief and social
> mileau. Such knowledge may or may not be true, but either way, it bears the

mark of its time and place. . . . The formulations of theology itself, while dealing with some abiding verities, are increasingly recognized as products of time and place.[5]

Lyon also suggests that "a little relativism, used the right way, is a handy cure for social scientific dogmatism and overreaching claims . . . too much relativism, as we shall see, is counter-productive."[6] This statement seems to regard relativism like salt in the kitchen: put a little in this dish, not too much in that one, and so on. But the question that always seems to be ignored is bypassed here also. Whether the consequences of relativism are perceived to be good or bad, the important question remains: is it true? Does it accurately describe the nature of human knowledge? If it is true, we cannot use a little here or there. Similarly, if it is false, we dare not use it at all.

This ambiguity, I would hypothesize, largely originates in fear. While some can simply reject relativism without thought, others recognize that there are relativistic aspects to human knowledge. Kraft echoed a widely perceived feeling when he wrote:

> There is fear that, if we once admit that God's revelations are conditioned by culture, we will not be logically able to stop short of the totally naturalistic perspective that has led many liberals to question the very existence of God.[7]

This line of reasoning is sometimes referred to as the "slippery slope" fallacy. It avoids the issue of truth by creating a fear that if people take one step in a certain direction, they will start sliding and never be able to return. It is widely used by fundamentalists and is a powerful deterrent. If all of one's religion and eternal soul is endangered by thinking about relativism—it is indeed a fearful matter. Conversely, if we fail to consider that possibility, there remains the lingering suspicion that there is a truth out there we are afraid to encounter.

Absolutists urge that all should seek knowledge of the Bible, and our approach will do just this. We will ask what the Bible says about human knowledge and the questions posed by relativity. In doing so we will use the principles of biblical interpretations used by absolutists.

The Bible has for many years been subjected to critical treatment by scholars who applied theories to it that were derived from the scientific spirit. Textual and higher criticism were refined and supplemented by other approaches. These have repeatedly called into question the authority of the Bible as revelation. That the people who believe the Bible to be God's word would not welcome such assaults is understandable. However, for the purpose of this study, these issues are irrelevant.

Three basic and related principles are assumed in the interpretation of the Bible made here. The first is that the text of the Bible should be accepted as it stands. Higher criticism, textual criticism, and other types of textual study are not taken into account. The absolutist Christian who buys a protestant Bible believes that what is purchased is a copy of the Word of God. This belief will not be challenged here. We will not attack the Bible's authenticity or authority in any way. We will assume as a basic principle the traditional belief that the Bible is God's Word.

The reader who disagrees with this assumption is asked to suspend that point temporarily. By taking for granted that the Bible is God's message, we can focus upon the absolutist or relativistic nature of the biblical text and bypass other issues.

The second principle is that the Bible represents a unity of thought. That is, it does not contradict itself. This does not mean that this assumption is a dogma for the study. If contradictions are found, they will be noted. What it does mean is that there is an underlying expectation of unity, and that which seems to be discrepant will be examined to see if there is a reasonable interpretation which resolves the disagreement. The bias will be toward unity rather than toward an expectation that unity will be lacking.

The third principle is that the text is authoritative. That is, in understanding the Bible, it is assumed that what the Bible teaches is the most important factor. If the Bible seems to say something that is unacceptable, it is not dismissed because it is unacceptable. The single question to be kept in mind is to determine as much as possible what it is the Bible states.

In questioning the relationship of the Bible to cultural relativity several questions will be explored: What does the Bible reveal about how God reveals truth? How is the pluralism of cultures dealt with in the Bible? What does the Bible teach about those who have different views of truth? What does the Bible teach about those who know nothing of Judaism or Christianity? Does biblical teaching include a relativistic dimension?

In this chapter these questions will be considered from the stance of a more general preliminary question: is the revelation of God as portrayed in the Bible more consistent with what one would expect in a world of absolutes or in a world of cultural relativity? Such a question is obviously somewhat speculative. It is not offered as a substitute for the work of the following chapters when the biblical text itself will be closely examined.

A Look at Revelation

Absolutists perceive God's message to be in statements that are to be believed because God has pronounced them. They hold that on each occasion of revelation, God gave an absolute message that those who were "God's people" received. This interpretation is considered to be self-evident and is asserted as an article of faith not requiring evidence.

On the other hand, the theory of cultural relativity would suggest that if revelation occurred it would require, if it were to be accepted, a long-term process in which a culture would develop among a people who would provide a social context for belief in the revelation. As this culture became established, it might be further influenced by additional revelations. All such revelations would take into account the existing state of that human culture. Thus their content and style might change as the culture evolved. This culture would have to compete with others in the pluralism of the world setting. It would often be influenced by the other cultures as well as influencing them. The implementation of revelation would require centuries in its cultural development to the point where it would be internalized as reality within a culture.

Cultural relativism can never deny revelation. What it can say is that if it has occurred, it must have come to be known by humans. Thus it must be subject to the relative characteristics of human knowledge. Cultural relativism, then, identifies the type of processes necessary for revelation wherever it might occur. The differences between revelation in a world where knowledge is absolute and one where it is relative is considerable.

In the practice of evaluating theories, we can unfortunately never find the conclusive and incontrovertible evidence we desire. What we can do is compare the fit between hypothesis and reality. If we find a lack of "fit," we know there is good reason either to modify or discard the theory. But if we find that the theory does fit, we can at least be intrigued and look for more information. It is this latter which I am suggesting here.

Does the biblical account of revelation fit with the principles of cultural relativity? I have been drawn to the conclusion that it fits very well. This conclusion was unexpected, and I do not expect it to appear persuasive to others without careful thought. It is too contrary to customary thinking. It was this conclusion which impelled me to examine the biblical text carefully. The result of that exploration will be explained in the next three chapters. What follows is a brief survey of the "fit" that led me to realize that the biblical text should be carefully examined.

The Bible states that after a great flood, God embarked on a new course in relating to humanity. This plan took approximately nineteen hundred years to complete. It began with Abraham, but instead of the absolutist revelation we might expect, it consisted of promises: a land, numerous descendants, and through these descendants, a blessing to all people of the world. It is unclear from the account what truths or norms Abraham considered to be a part of his religion. But it is clear that Abraham, about nineteen hundred years before Christ, took with him a small clan of people and left his native land and culture.

The elements were in place for the emergence of a new culture. Abraham and his clan had left their native culture to live in relative isolation. The danger of not isolating oneself from the cultural environment was demonstrated in the error of Lot, who chose to live in an already populated city. God's promise was undeniably long-term. Instead of many descendants, Abraham had only one, who was considered a recipient of the promise. And that son had only two sons.

As a grandfather, Abraham could not have cited much empirical evidence of a massive number of descendants. The biblical interpretation was that it took nineteen hundred years for the development of the nation and its culture to progress to the point of the advent of the Messiah.

Whatever the beliefs and norms of Abraham's religion were, they seem to have been much different from those which were evident in later Christian thought. Perhaps Abraham and Sarah were wrong in their "sexual experimentation" in attempting to have a son. This does not seem to have been considered a matter of falling into temptation, however, but something that seemed a matter of course to them. Though the results were not happy, there is no suggestion in the record that they had broken any "religious rule."

I mention this because it is important not to read the Bible backwards. That is, it should not be assumed that what later Jews knew about God was what Abraham knew. There is ample testimony that Abraham was a man of great faith. But there is no evidence that he had an understanding of God that resembled what was later evident in the law of Moses. Why not? If revelation can be absolute, a man of faith would accept the teachings. But if it is relative, it would mean that though Abraham was a man of faith, he simply did not have the cultural context to understand and implement God's revelation as would people in later times.

The giving of the law at Mount Sinai several centuries after the promise to Abraham made explicit a set of rules and regulations for what was, by then, the promised massive number of descendants. Though these comprised a large nation, there was no suggestion in the revelation that the promised blessing of the world had occurred. Indeed, many more centuries passed. The nation often failed to follow these laws. It was divided and conquered. The worship of idols was prevalent. When destroyed and made captive by Babylon, it appeared that the nation would be assimilated, as had happened to most ancient nations. The nation was never a powerful force except for a few years at best. Mostly, it was a pawn in the power plays of the mighty nations around it. As captives in Babylon, the descendants of Abraham wept, but they also taught their traditions to their children. The return to their native land finally occurred. Throughout this history stretching over centuries of time there is clearly a development of the Jewish culture. Catastrophic events occurred but the culture emerged with new strengths.

In the New Testament there is the intriguing idea that the coming of Christ was "in the fullness of time."[8] Much has been written to support the notion that the political and social conditions were exactly right for the time in which Christ appeared. It has also been noted that technology had developed in an advantageous way so that ship travel had increased and the Roman roads facilitated travel. Whatever the precise conditions were, the early Christians saw it as the end of the very long process that had begun nineteen centuries earlier.

Another element is important to note: Jesus lived within that Jewish culture.

He taught and worshiped within it. He referred to it for authoritative support for his teachings. That he gave new dimensions to it is evident. Yet his teachings were always within the context of Judaism. We sometimes say that Jesus was rejected by the Jews, but that statement is a misinterpretation. Those who rejected him were Jews, but so were those who accepted and followed him. So also were the three thousand who were baptized on the first Pentecost of the church as well as the additional thousands who soon after were baptized. Among the leading rulers of the Jews, many accepted the validity of Jesus' message.[9] The point is that Jesus' experience was the culmination of a plan that took nineteen centuries during which a unique society and culture developed.

The biblical message is consistent with what cultural relativity suggests would be the nature of revelation if it were to occur. If it were possible to institute a cultural absolute that could have been effective, it would not have required nineteen centuries. Generations of people from Abraham to Christ would have benefited. The interpretation that I am proposing is that the Christian message was itself a culture. It was an expression of the earlier culture that developed in Judaism and originated with the call of Abraham. And it was in this way that Abraham became known as the father of the faith.[10] The Jews of Jesus' day knew their cultural origins came from Abraham. It was the meaning of this culture that characterized discussion between the Jews and Jesus.[11]

This culture of God has mingled with other cultures and sometimes seemed to have been overwhelmed by them. But it has survived as a definition of reality with a set of beliefs, norms, and values that continues to call humans to its particular point of view. Any revelation God could make would have to be placed in a cultural context. The relativity of human knowledge requires this, and the revelation of Christ was delayed for many centuries while God nurtured that cultural base in Judaism.

It is in this line of thought that a curious reversal of our situation has taken place. Cultural relativity originally was thought to be the enemy of the faith. It was to be feared as undercutting truth. Yet, the enemy may now begin to look like a friend. Relativity contains nothing that can destroy the idea that God revealed himself through the prophets and Jesus. It can identify the process through which biblical revelation is portrayed in the Bible. But it does more than this. Cultural relativism also makes us aware that what any age believes to be "self-evident" may be persuasive only because of its cultural context. When applied, it will call into question any simplistic assumptions that what passes for knowledge in our contemporary culture is necessarily superior to other cultures at other times.

The Reality of Internalized Culture

Three initial concepts prove important in understanding biblical religion as the story of the development of a culture. The first concept is that of internalized culture: a cultural trait has been internalized when it has become a part of the personality. For example, the individual who refuses to litter, though sure that no one would know the difference, has a personality that has internalized the norm of not littering. When internalized, a trait is a powerful factor in one's life and exerts control. Its truth and value usually seem self-evident and beyond question.

A curious experience occurs in the attempt to understand and teach culture. When you see it, it really is not there and when you do not see it, it is there. A cultural trait that is truly internalized in my personality seems to be so self-evidently true that it is difficult for me to recognize it as cultural and not some absolute reality. Those matters that come to mind as being aspects of culture probably are not fully internalized in the personality. It is because they are not fully internalized that they can be easily used as examples of culture. Yet, because they are not internalized, they also do not seem to be very powerful. For example, sex roles are often used as examples in sociology classes, because people are aware that there are alternative definitions of them. Students today are not very likely to have internalized a clearly defined set of sex roles and therefore understand such examples readily. If, however, I suggest that the concept of equal pay for both sexes for equal work is also a cultural definition, there will be students who become incensed. They see this as an unquestionable standard of fairness and do not understand how any person of "good will" could have believed that the male as family provider should be paid more than the working woman. It is difficult for them to accept that their concept of equal pay for equal work is not a matter of absolute fairness but a concept that has been internalized into their thinking. To repeat, the norms that are really internalized are powerful influences over behavior and are perceived by the individual to be beyond reasonable question. The traits we easily identify as cultural tend to be those that are not internalized and therefore not very powerful in affecting us.

When viewed in this manner, an additional consideration is suggested: firm Christian faith is likely to make an acceptance of cultural relativity difficult to adopt. Similarly, a firm faith in social science is likely to make it easy for the sociologist to neglect to recognize the relativity of social science. But it will be easy for the social scientist to be aware of the cultural relativity of the Christian faith. Similarly, it will be easy for the Christian to observe such inconsistency by the social scientists. The willingness to accept either Christian belief or cultural relativity is, to some degree, a measure of which cultural traits have already been internalized into the personality.

This characteristic means that even the choice of examples poses a problem in that what is a good example for some will not be for others. Perhaps the examples already given will be accurate for purposes of illustration. Perhaps not. The point must not be obscured: internalized cultural traits are real and have real consequences. Shakespeare's character was wrong when he said that there was "nothing good or bad but thinking makes it so." Instead, what a culture defines as good is internalized into the personality and becomes a powerful determinant of perceptions and behavior. Cultural relativists see culture as a powerful definer of truth and not as subjective, individual thought.

Ethnocentrism and Chronocentrism

The other two concepts to be explored are ethnocentrism and chronocentrism. The power of internalized cultural traits to seem self-evidently true is a basic component of ethnocentrism—that characteristic stance in which one's own group or society is seen as inherently superior to others. The traits of one's culture seem more factual and moral than do traits of other cultures. But ethnocentrism can also operate chronologically. That is, what is internalized from the culture in which one is currently socialized seems inherently more appealing, moral, and factual than any concepts of cultures which one may know of from the past. To illustrate, the styles of dress currently in fashion have a certain appeal, whereas photographs of people from the past probably look strange, awkward, stiff, and unappealing. Students wonder how people in the past could have had such rigid sex roles or how it could have seemed fair to pay men more than women for the same job. Though there is some nostalgia for the past, it is limited compared to the whole range of current cultural phenomena that seem superior to the past. To be chronocentric is to judge the past by the standards of the present. It is to do with history what ethnocentrism does in the understanding of other cultures. Peter Berger identified this chronocentrism well:

> All share the conviction that modern man stands on some sort of cognitive pinnacle, from which he can survey and overcome the shortcomings of all his predecessors. . . . Is it not possible that, while modern man has gained some valid insights into reality, he has also lost some equally valid insights?[12]

To raise this point is to call into question the current cultural reality. It is to reduce our current view to only one in a long list of ways of looking at reality. It is, in other words, to make relative the current way of seeing the world. Our current view is thus not necessarily the pinnacle but is relative to the particular situation in which we live. It seems like the pinnacle because we have internalized it and use it as the standard for comparison. Once we realize the power of chronocentrism, all of the worlds of reality seem changed. Christian, Communist, or scientific—the worlds are all changed since each is a product of an evolving culture which shapes its perceptions of truth. Berger summarizes this by referring to the view of reality as a "structure of consciousness."

> History brings forth and dissolves one structure of consciousness after another. Each one is to be taken seriously and looked at in terms of its

possible insights. In this respect, modern consciousness is one among many historically available structures—no more, no less. To see the matter in this way precludes any apodictic statements as to what modern men "can no longer" believe. In this as in many other matters, historical understanding and the sociology of knowledge conspire to produce a healthy skepticism about the taken-for-granted certainties of any age, one's own included.[13]

A characteristic of the modern world is that all individuals face increased numbers of choices. Not only are there more brands of breakfast cereals from which to choose, there are more options in sex roles, there are options in psychotherapies, and there are increasingly more options in medical treatment. There are, of course, the much publicized "life-style options" that can be taken to include choices in beliefs. This pluralism, Berger reminds us, is "ipso facto a weakening of every conceivable belief and value dependent upon social support."[14]

> The modern individual must engage in more deliberate thinking—not because he is more intelligent, not because he is on some sort of higher level of consciousness, but because his social situation forces him to this.[15]

When there are alternate versions of reality we are less sure which is the better truth. The cultural effect of this inevitably will be the creation of uncertainty. To hold on to clear-cut beliefs that lack social support will demand a price in defense mechanisms. It will force one to appear more certain than one really is. Or one must be resigned to the notion that truth is unknowable. For what we have learned about culture is crucial: humans cannot simply choose whatever they wish to be right or wrong. We are always subject to the "historical situation."[16]

Our current culture is a product of development just as are others. It is not a pinnacle, though it may seem like one to any who are socialized into the "modern" world. There are elements of knowledge available—especially the cause and effect relationships of a vast number of variables through science—that were unknown in the past. But there are also many facts known in the past that have been lost. We are part of this process, and our own socialization experiences have equally shaped us. Our own epistemologies are similarly a part of the larger social processes of the place and time in which we live.

It is precisely the failure to recognize the relativity of culture that leads contemporaries to believe that there could really be no useful truth gained from a movement based on events which occurred almost two thousand years ago among the Jews. What could they know without modern science? An appreciation of cultural relativity can be a first step toward rooting out these ethnocentric and chronocentric prejudices that make up so much of modern consciousness. It appropriately causes us to consider the possibility that cultures in other times and places that were quite different from ours also could have important truths. That this idea is so foreign to our mode of thought is evidence of how ethnocentric and chronocentric our thinking is. Indeed, is it not true that we conventionally believe that people of other lands and times provide no knowledge from which we can benefit? On what basis do we think this? There is none except our chronocentric and ethnocentric contemporary culture.

A major stumbling block in considering that there may be truth in biblical religion is that it is so old and foreign. It is in this that cultural relativity, instead of being a threat to Christianity, can be a considerable benefit. Contemporary consciousness is subject to its own versions of ethnocentrism and chrono-centrism, and this powerful impact is shaken when we become conscious of it. There is no reason to automatically discount ideas from ancient documents such as the Bible except for our chronocentrism. A conscious and critical appreciation for cultural relativism need not undermine biblical revelation, but it should call into question the hold contemporary consciousness has over our ways of thinking.

Defensiveness against cultural relativism and assertions of absolutism do not aid the church. We live in a world where the pluralism of the "small, small world" increasingly intrudes upon our understanding. This pluralism forces a certain cultural relativism on the consciousness of increasing numbers of people. In the village of the past where the culture was more homogeneous, the church could call upon a common heritage to attempt to secure the commitment of members. In this setting, ethnocentric and chronocentric views could be very appealing. In a pluralistic neighborhood, a different strategy must be utilized.

A case can also be made that the contemporary ethnocentric and chrono-centric views among social scientists do not aid science. Indeed, sociology tends to ignore even its own classics, regarding them as obsolete though they are less than a century old! And then, as Buford Rhea noted, "We typically organize sociology curricula so that students are virtually informed that the classics are now irrelevant."[17] The social philosophers of all previous ages seem to be almost totally ignored. Material utilized for research is almost completely the recent work of American sociologists. The ethnocentrism and chronocentrism of current American sociology is antithetical to the concern sociologists express over the ethnocentrism of others. Sociology's approach would seem to preclude any serious consideration of Christianity on anything other than a patronizing basis. Yet this characteristic is not found only in social science but in the broader culture of our society. We seem to be a "now generation," not only because we do not defer gratification for the future, but also because we ignore the past. Relativity is a powerful force for uncovering these hidden assumptions in our culture.

The argument I have tried to make here takes a preliminary step toward answering the question raised at the first of the chapter. It makes explicit two conclusions. First, the process of revelation over the nineteen centuries from Abraham to Christ is consistent with what cultural relativity would suggest to be necessary. This process would not have been necessary if truth could be understood as absolute.

The second conclusion is that cultural relativism does call into question the ethnocentric and chronocentric beliefs so prevalent in both contemporary social science and culture. There is nothing inherently improbable in the possibility that people in a far-off age and place could have important insights from which we can benefit, except that our ethnocentric and chronocentric biases exclude it. We have no basis for considering the probability of a revelation. But if it were to happen, there is no reason to believe that it could not just as well have been two thousand years ago as five hundred years ago or next year. Our tendency to think otherwise is simple chronocentrism.

8

Old Testament Documents

> The Lord, the God of your fathers—the God of Abraham, the
> God of Isaac and the God of Jacob . . . This is my name forever.
> —Exodus 3 : 15

We now examine the text of the Bible with the issue of relativity in mind: does the biblical text support the view of cultural relativity or are they irreconcilable? Just as the ideas of relativity developed out of cross-cultural studies, so also we are likely to gain insight in those biblical situations where pluralism was present.

The biblical passages are considered in the order in which they appear in the Bible. Some will be more important for the main issues and others will be less so. For some passages, the interpretation may be different from that with which the reader has understood them in the past. New questions occasion new approaches and may result in new interpretations. I do not ask the reader to accept them without careful consideration. I do ask that the interpretations not be rejected merely because they may not be conventional.

The Old Testament begins "in the beginning" and spans the centuries up to the era preceding the life of Jesus. Its thirty-nine documents are arranged into three historical eras: the period before the Hebrew nation developed, the history of that nation, and the later period of its decline and reestablishment. These three sections are called the patriarchal, nationhood, and late prophetic periods.

The Patriarchal Age

The first section of the Old Testament—often identified as the patriarchal age—begins with statements about the creation of the world. It closes with the emergence of the Hebrews as an independent nation that escaped from Egyptian domination while under the leadership of Moses. This event has traditionally been dated at about 1500 B.C.

The opening words of the Old Testament portray a God who is the God of the universe—not a tribal deity, but the originator of everything, and a deity who held conversations with the first humans. In these conversations between the creator and the created humans there was a common cultural bond. That is, they shared understandings of symbols—words—that made conversation possible and presupposed the existence of a common culture, at least to some extent. Deviance from that culture occurred early when Adam and Eve succumbed to the serpent's tempting.[1] The emergence of different cultures—different kinds of people—also appeared with the identification of the "sons of God" and the "daughters of men."[2] The conflict between these cultures was so great and the violence of the counter-culture so prevalent that God sent a flood to destroy the wickedness of the counter-culture.[3]

Following the flood, language differences appeared at Babel,[4] and from that time on, the record is clear that there were diverse peoples with disparate cultures. The questions of cultural relativity that we are asking become applicable with the existence of these distinct cultural groups.

This period as a whole is something of a shadowy era for which the specific beliefs and religious practices are impossible to ascertain. Similarly, how they regarded other cultures and the religions of other cultures is unknown. Nevertheless, the Bible records five events in this period that do give us very fragmentary insight. Whether these can be generalized as revealing the practice of the period cannot be determined. They do provide some basic understanding for events that occurred later.

The first of these is the call of Abraham. This was the fundamental event for the Jewish religion, and in it is the original base for the Christian faith. Expressed in a different way, if this event were removed from all knowledge, a gap in the explanation of the origin of the Judeo-Christian tradition would be evident. A loss of information about the earlier events would result in a lack of understanding but would not be as significant a loss. The Jewish people, including Jesus and the apostles, spoke of Abraham as the father of the faith. God's call to Abraham was simple and straightforward:

> Go from your country and your kindred and your father's house to the land that I will show you. And I will make of you a great nation, and I will bless you, and make your name great so that you will be a blessing. I will bless those who bless you, and him who curses you I will curse; and by you all the families of the earth, will bless themselves.[5]

In this original promise to Abraham there are two themes that are consistently followed—that God is both particular and universal. That is, Abraham, and his descendants who became the Hebrew nation, were a specific people chosen by God who was their deity. In this way the religion was never a general principle, but always a particular set of events to a particular group of people. But the religion's ultimate objective was not limited to one people or nation but to the whole population of the world. All families will be able to bless themselves, it was promised, because of this relationship between God and Abraham. This includes, but is not limited to, Abraham's descendants. In the importance of

understanding Abraham, we must not lose sight of this promise that was for "all
the families of the earth." Though God was the deity of the Hebrews, this was
not an end in itself, but a means to a universal purpose: the benefit of all people.

This promise to Abraham, according to Christian interpretation, set in
motion a process that would last nineteen hundred years and result in the
ministry of Christ. It would in its course create a people of God—a culture—that
would verify and establish God's truth. As I asserted in the last chapter, if truth
is relative and must be based in a culture, this long process of revelation would be
necessary. In making the promise, God instructed Abraham to leave his homeland and the family of his birth. He was thus to be isolated from the culture of his
birth and to be a "sojourner in a strange land" for the rest of his life. This also
was a necessary prerequisite for the development of a new culture.

A second situation concerns Abraham's grandson Jacob and provides a glimpse
at the issue of pluralism and how other religions were regarded. When Abraham's grandson, Jacob, was ready to marry, he returned to Abraham's homeland
to find a wife—to the culture that Abraham had left. Jacob lived there twenty-
one years as part of the arrangement to marry Rachel. When Jacob had married
and left with his family to return to the land where Abraham had settled, Rachel
stole the household gods of her father.[6] He recognized that they had been stolen
and searched Jacob's tent, though he did not find them. In the conversation
about this it is evident that the issue for Jacob was one of stolen property and not
of religious truth.[7] No suggestion is made that the gods were untrue, but neither
was there any suggestion that possession of these gods was of any meaning other
than the concern for the question of ownership.

The third case also involves Jacob at a later period in his life. His daughter,
Dinah, was raped by a Shechemite—a non-Hebrew—who wanted to marry her.[8]
Jacob's sons deceitfully acted as if the marriage would be arranged, and under this
ruse found an opportunity to kill the males of the Schechemite family. Jacob
feared that this would cause the Schechemites to form a coalition with others
against his family.[9] It was at this time that God told Jacob to move his family to
Bethel, dwell there, and build an altar. In the process of carrying out this order,
Jacob called on the family to abandon their "foreign gods," purify themselves,
and change their garments.[10]

Was the command for purification a part of the elimination of foreign gods, or
was it a separate commandment? The answer is not apparent. But it is clear that
the foreign gods had been a part of the household, but they were now unacceptable. The nature of the gods, the reality they represented, and why some
members of Jacob's family possessed them, was not revealed.

The fourth example concerns Joseph, the son of Jacob. Joseph was separated
from his family and ended up in jail in Egypt, where through a series of events he
was made second in command to Pharoah and was given authority to administer
the nation's food program. Joseph created vast storage facilities for grain. When
famine came and the people of Egypt ran out of food, he sold them food in

exchange for the title to their land. During the course of the seven years of famine, Joseph was able to buy all of the land of Egypt from the people and secure title to it for Pharoah. It boggles the mind to consider the response if such a policy were attempted today in our country. There must have been much opposition to it by many people in Egypt. In spite of this, Joseph successfully completed the transfer of all of the property of the nation into Pharoah's ownership.

There was only one exception to this policy. Joseph did not buy up the land which belonged to the Egyptian priests.[11] They were granted a stipend from the government that allowed them to do what no one else could do—buy food from Joseph while maintaining title to their land. With all of his power, Joseph did not challenge the special interests of the Egyptian priests though everyone else in the nation became propertyless. The reason for this is unknown. But it is clear that though Joseph is portrayed as faithful to his own religion, he did not question the standing of the religion of the Egyptians.

The last example concerns Moses. By his time the descendants of Abraham had become a great number of people, but they were enslaved in Egypt. God called Moses to be their leader and bring about their escape from Egypt. Moses did not welcome this call, and in his indecision asked a question which was crucial:

> If I come to the people of Israel and say to them, "The God of your fathers has sent me to you" and they ask me, "What is his name?" what shall I say to them?[12]

God gives two answers to this question:

> I am who I am . . . Say this to the people of Israel, "I am has sent me to you."
> Say this to the people of Israel, "The Lord, the God of Abraham, the God of Isaac, and the God of Jacob has sent me to you." This is my name for ever, and thus I am to be remembered throughout all generations.[13]

In these two answers the theme of God as both universal and particular is explicit. God asserts a certain universalism in his response that "he is." Much has been made of this—and much should be made of it—this simple declaration of being. Existence itself is given as the identity of a creator-being, God.

The second answer ties this universal-theological statement to a particular set of historical events. It reaffirms what Moses suggested in his question—that God was the God of their ancestors: Abraham, his son, and his grandson. God's answer affirms this. Moses was to tell them that it was the God of Abraham, Isaac, and Jacob who had established Moses' leadership and the rightfulness of their escape from slavery. But God also revealed to Moses that in all future generations this was to be his name. It would remain important that God would be designated not just in terms of universal being but also in terms of the particular events in the lives of Abraham, his son, and his grandson. God was revealed to be both universal and also known through a particular group of people and the culture of that people.

To draw any conclusions from these five events is impossible. Yet they do suggest at least a possible interpretation. There were other religions and other deities. There was no evident need to discredit them or to proclaim their falseness. They were simpy regarded as there. They were, however, to have no part in the lives of the children of Abraham. The institutions of other religions were not disturbed even when, in the case of Joseph, he probably had the power to do so. The children of Abraham were the people of God, though God was not a tribal but a universal deity. God was creating a people and a culture through which his truth could be known.

The Era of Nationhood

With the giving of the law on Mount Sinai, the Israelites began to function as a nation. The law was built around ten basic commandments and the first of these concerned other gods. This first commandment was unequivocal:

> You shall have no other gods before me. You shall not make yourself a graven image, or any likeness of anything that is in heaven above, or that is in the earth beneath, or that is in the water under the earth; you shall not bow down to them or serve them; for I the Lord your God am a jealous God, visiting the iniquity of the fathers upon the children to the third and the fourth generation of those who hate me, but showing steadfast love to thousands of those who love me and keep my commandments.[14]

To this basic law was added several other laws which elaborated it:

> Whoever sacrifices to any god, save to the Lord only, shall be utterly destroyed.[15]
> Take heed to all that I have said to you; and make no mention of the names of other gods, nor let such be heard out of your mouth.[16]
> You shall make no covenant with (the inhabitants of the promised land) or with their gods. They shall not dwell in your land, lest they make you sin against me; for if you serve their gods, it will surely be a snare to you.[17]

When the Israelites occupied the land God had promised to them, they were to destroy all of the gods completely and all of the people as well.[18] The reason for the destruction of the people was the danger their religions posed for the Israelites:

> But you shall utterly destroy them . . . that they may not teach you to do according to all their abominable practices which they have done in the service of their gods, and so to sin against the Lord your God.[19]

In establishing their nation, the destruction of other religions clearly had the highest priority. This destruction was to be carried out not only among the other people but also among the Israelites. If any of the Israelites "served other gods and worshiped them, or the sun or the moon or any of the host of heaven . . . [they were to] stone that man or woman to death with stones."[20] The same would be true for any prophet who would suggest that the people should follow other gods.[21]

If the Israelites followed other gods in spite of these laws, the book of Leviticus detailed God's promise of punishment:

> I will walk contrary to you in fury, and chastise you myself sevenfold for your sins. You shall eat the flesh of your sons, and you shall eat the flesh of your daughters. And I will destroy your high places and cut down your incense altars, and cast your dead bodies upon the dead bodies of your idols; and my soul will abhor you. And I will lay your cities waste, and will make your sanctuaries desolate, and I will not smell your pleasing odors. And I will devastate the land, so that your enemies who settle in it shall be astonished at it. And I will scatter you among the nations, and I will unsheathe the sword after you; and your land shall be a desolation, and your cities shall be a waste.[22]

In spite of these laws and the promise of punishment, the text indicates that the Israelites continued to worship other gods. Joshua stated that Abraham's father had served "other gods,"[23] but God had separated Abraham from him apparently so that he could avoid that practice. The Israelites, however, continued in it.[24] After escaping from Egypt they worshiped Egyptian gods.[25] Later they adopted the worship of the gods of the Canaanites, Syrians, Sidonians, Moabites, Ammonites, and Philistines.[26]

The Israelites proved to be truly eclectic in their religion. King Solomon married wives from various nations who enticed him to accept the worship of various gods.[27] Later Jereboam thought that it was necessary to permit the worship of these gods if he were to keep the loyalty of the nation.[28] The extent of these practices by the Israelites is shocking:

> And the people of Israel did secretly against the Lord their God things that were not right. They built for themselves high places at all their towns, from watchtower to fortified city; they set up for themselves pillars and Asherim on every high hill and under every green tree, and they burned incense on all the high places as the nations did . . . they served idols . . . They despised [God's] statutes, and his covenant. . . . They went after false idols, and became false, and they followed the nations that were round about them . . . they made for themselves molten images of two calves; and they made an Asherah, and worshiped all the host of heaven, and served Baal. And they burned their sons and their daughters as offerings, and used divination and sorcery, and sold themselves to do evil in the sight of the Lord, provoking him to anger. Therefore the Lord was very angry with

Israel, and removed them out of his sight; none was left but the tribe of Judah only.[29]

These details provide several important considerations. The Law of Moses had as a central principle that the Israelites were to have nothing to do with any other religion. The people, however, persisted in disobeying this law, though there were numerous times when reform was attempted. Finally, the destruction which God had promised happened. It would become evident later on that of the remnant of the Jews who survived, this persistence in worshiping other gods was removed.

But what view did the Old Testament writers present about these "other gods"? Repeatedly, they were referred to in the warnings to the Israelites to avoid them. But their existence was seldom questioned. They were spoken of as if they existed as something more than the material images that represented them. Even the basic commandment that states, "you shall have no other gods before me," seems to imply that there were other gods.

Instead, the Israelites were told that their relationship was with God—the God of Abraham, Isaac, and Jacob, the one who had brought them out of bondage in Egypt. He also was the creator and he had a covenant with them.[30] God was identified in terms of his revealed characteristics rather than in terms that denied the existence of all others. Repeatedly, the reality of other gods was stated in the Old Testament without any question having been raised concerning their existence.

There were a few times where statements were made that may indicate an awareness that the other gods were nonexistent. In Moses' spoken law, there was a prediction that the Israelites would serve other gods. These would be "gods of wood and stone, the work of men's hands, that neither see nor hear nor eat nor smell."[31] To us this probably seems to be a clear statement that these gods were not real deities. But the indications are quite clear that to the people of that time, this would not have been their interpretation. The Israelites knew that the gods they worshiped in the wilderness were made by human hands, but they worshiped them just the same.[32] As impossible as it may be for us to understand, the ancient people did not have difficulty with the idea that the idol they made with their own hands could become a god of power to be worshiped. The meaning of this statement would seem to be that the God of the Israelites was superior to the other gods in these characteristics, rather than a declaration that the others were false.

This interpretation is consistent with the context. He continued:

Did any people ever hear the voice of a god speaking out of the midst of the fire, as you have heard, and still live? Or has any god ever attempted to go and take a nation for himself from the midst of another nation, by trials, by signs, by wonders, and by war . . . To you it was shown, that you might know that the Lord is God; there is no other besides him.[33]

Does this mean that there is no other god or that there is no other god who is equal? Moses added another statement relevant to this in his presentation: "For the Lord your God is God of gods and Lord of lords, the great, the mighty, and the terrible God."[34] A clear meaning is that there was no god who was equal to the God of the Israelites who could hear, see, and speak. No other god had the power to act as he had demonstrated. Therefore he had no equal. In the context in which the other gods were spoken of as if they were real, and in which the God of the Israelites was termed the "God of gods," the reality of the other gods was not denied.

A second instance when such a denial of the existence of other gods might have been indicated was when Gideon destroyed some of the idols that were being worshiped. When the townspeople came to punish him, his father defended Gideon by saying of the destroyed god, "If he is a god let him contend for himself because his altar has been pulled down."[35] This theme was repeated under a later judge where God spoke to the Israelites: "Go and cry to the gods whom you have chosen; let them deliver you in the time of your distress."[36]

Another event continues this same line of argument. It happened when Elijah challenged the gods on Mount Carmel.[37] The prophets of the gods were to try to get their gods to send fire to consume the sacrifices on the altar. When this failed, Elijah prayed to the God of the Israelites to burn the sacrifices, and this occurred. The purpose was stated in Elijah's prayer:

> O Lord, God of Abraham, Isaac, and Israel, let it be known this day that thou art God in Israel, and that I am thy servant, and that I have done all these things at thy word.[38]

The prayer defines the scope. Elijah was concerned with the worship of the Israelites—that they see that God was the only god for them and was a god of power. It was not an effort to establish that other religions were false. It seems similar to Elijah's response when Ahaziah sent messengers to the god of Ekron to ask about his chances of recovery from an accident. Elijah's question was, "Is it because there is no God in Israel that you are going to inquire of Baalsebub, the God of Ekron?[39] Again these are not conclusive statements that the other religions were considered to be false. A passage already cited, 2 Kings 17:15, makes a reference to "false idols." This may be a reference that all are false. Its specific statement is that the people at that time worshiped idols that were false, but it makes no assertion about all idols. It is very clear that Israelites were commanded not to worship other gods, and that the God of Israel was considered to be a more powerful and responsive God—the God of gods. Why the people persisted in worshiping the other gods was not discussed in the Old Testament.

By the late prophetic period it is evident that the idols were believed to be false. The point remains that for centuries the worship of the other gods was condemned without any unambiguous statements that they were not gods. I know of no way of determining why this was so. The thrust of the law and the prophets was to keep the Israelites away from the worship of these other gods. It was never to attempt to convince other people that their gods were not real. There is no evidence that they used absolutist statements as this term is used today.

It is also clear that differences of belief were considered to be very important. The era in which the Hebrew nation emerged, prospered, and fell was one that demonstrated both an acceptance of diverse cultural definitions and also an assertion of the importance of the Israelites' beliefs.

It was in the era of national decline that for the first time unequivocal statements were made that there were no other gods than the God of Abraham. Isaiah, whose writings are dated at the earliest as being from the late seventh or early sixth century before Christ made several such statements:

> Can man make for himself gods? Such are no gods.[40]
>
> Has a nation changed its gods, even though they are no gods? But my people have changed their glory for that which does not profit.[41]
>
> Hear the word which the Lord speaks to you, O house of Israel. Thus says the Lord: Learn not the way of the nations, nor be dismayed at the signs of the heavens because the nations are dismayed at them, for the customs of the peoples are false. A tree from the forest is cut down, and worked with an axe by the hands of a craftsman. Men deck it with silver and gold; they fasten it with hammer and nails so that it cannot move. Their idols are like scarecrows in a cucumber field, and they cannot speak; they have to be carried, for they cannot walk. Be not afraid of them, for they cannot do evil, neither is it in them to do good. . . . They are both stupid and foolish; the instruction of idols is but wood!. . . . But the Lord is the true God; he is the living God and the everlasting King. At his wrath the earth quakes and the nations cannot endure his indignation.[42]

The dating of these documents is a matter of considerable controversy. The unequivocal declarations that idols were not gods, whatever the opinion on dates, was a late development. For centuries, the commandment had been to forbid the worship of other gods but the reality of these other gods was not denied. But there were other new ideas introduced in the later periods when the worship of idols disappeared among the Jews.

Late Prophetic Period

Several passages in the last eight books of the Old Testament seem to be related to the issue of cultural relativity and raise intriguing questions. They are found in a section of the Old Testament often referred to as the minor prophets—the label "minor" refers to the short length of the writings rather than to their level of importance.

The book of Jonah is unique in the Old Testament: it is not a pronouncement in which the prophet speaks for God to the people as are the other books.

Rather, it is a biographical account of an event in the life of the prophet himself. Jonah was given a prophetic message that was to be delivered not to Jewish people but to non-Jews—the people of Ninevah, the great Assyrian city. After fleeing in the opposite direction and being swallowed by the great fish, Jonah went to Nineveh and delivered the prophetic message that Nineveh would be destroyed unless the people repented.

What the people of Ninevah thought of Jonah as he went about the streets proclaiming this message is not stated. Neither is there any indication of what they knew or thought of the Jewish God Jehovah. The king, however, took the message seriously, issued the necessary edicts, and the city repented and was spared. This result was not what Jonah expected and he did not like it. The last part of the book tells of the plant that grew up, sheltered Jonah, and then withered away. This occurred so that God could provide a lesson to the prophet.

The book of Jonah, then, is an account of several incidents in which a prophetic message was delivered to a non-Jewish city and in which a major portion of the book is not about the prophet's message, but the work of God in instructing and changing the prophet himself. The book of Jonah charts a new course in Jewish prophecy. Its call for the repentance of non-Jews was difficult for Jonah to accept, as it undoubtedly was also for other Jewish people of Jonah's day.

The nature of the book suggests that it was directed to the Jewish people. The repentance of Nineveh had already occurred when it was written. The book, therefore, could not have been intended as a message to the Ninevites. Its purpose, instead, would seem to be to gain among the Jews a new understanding that God was the God of other nations and could also call them to his message. The book of Jonah was in the spirit of God's promise to Abraham that all of the peoples of the world would receive blessing.

In five of the seven books that are placed between the book of Jonah and the end of the Old Testament, there are interesting passages that also seem to follow the direction of thought explicit in Jonah. Such passages do not occur in books placed before Jonah, which may suggest a change of emphasis among the later prophets. When these passages are compared with Jesus' teachings, an interesting pattern occurs.

Three principles may be gained from the passages of the last Old Testament prophets. First, it was clearly stated that God was at work among other nations, not just among the Jews.

> Great is the Lord beyond the borders of Israel.[43]
> Look among the nations and see; wonder and be astounded. For I am doing a work in your days that you would not believe if told.[44]

Second, it was recognized that the nations worshiped their own gods.

> For all the peoples walk each in the name of its god, but we will walk in the name of the Lord our God for ever and ever.[45]

Third, the prophets announced that there would be a future time when these other nations would seek to learn about Jehovah.

> Many peoples and strong nations shall come to seek the Lord of hosts in Jerusalem, and to entreat the favor of the Lord. Thus says the Lord of hosts: In those days ten men from the nations of every tongue shall take hold of the robe of a Jew, saying, "Let us go with you, for we have heard that God is with you."[46]

Keeping in mind these ideas, we will now examine three additional passages. In looking at each I will consider what the text means and suggest an interpretation. The interpretations I am suggesting must be considered tentative. The interpretation of one passage may not prove the point. Taken as part of the biblical presentation as a whole, each of these steps can provide important insights. It is especially important to consider these in the light of the later teachings of Jesus and the apostles.

The first is from Zephaniah.

> Woe to her that is rebellious and defiled, the oppressing city! She listens to no voice, she accepts no correction. She does not trust in the Lord, she does not draw near to her God.[47]

The text identified Ethiopia and Nineveh—two non-Jewish cities—as the oppressors. Their condemnation was not only that they did not trust in Jehovah but also that they rejected their own god. It was of consequence in God's judgment that they were unfaithful to their god though that god was false. That is, God recognized as valuable that a people followed that which they perceived to be true. That the god was false did not mean that disobedience to that god was of no consequence. To care about and respond to what is perceived to be true was thus an important consideration in God's judgment. That is, God's judgment was relative to the cultural knowledge they possessed.

The second passage is from Malachi.

> For from the rising of the sun to its setting my name is great among the nations and in every place incense is offered to my name.[48]

Initially the meaning of this seems obvious. Throughout the world, according to the passage, there were people who worshiped God and offered incense in His name. Did this mean that there were Jewish proselytes throughout the nations at that time? A complicating factor for this interpretation is that it is difficult to believe that there were Jewish people this widely dispersed at that time or that there were proselytes in every place throughout the nations.

An alternative interpretation avoids this problem. It is that though people may have had no knowledge of the God of Abraham, yet, in their devotion to truth as they knew it, they were in some sense offering incense to Him. Stated in another way, those who followed the truth, as they knew it, had in common with those who followed the truth of Jehovah that they loved truth and sought to follow it. God recognized faithfulness to the truth, whatever the truth was perceived to be, as faithfulness to Him. This idea is a very tenuous interpretation when based only on this one passage.

The third passage is from Zechariah.

> And the Lord will become king over all the earth; on that day the Lord will be one and his name one.[49]

The apparent meaning is not so clear here. Was not the Lord God already one and his name one? Was not God already king over all the earth? How then could these things be an achievement of the future? An interpretation that provides an answer to these questions is that the prophetic message was speaking not about the nature of God, but the perception of God by the world. Thus it was saying that when the world recognizes the God of the Jews as the king of the world then there would be the recognition that there is one God and His name would be one. There is no suggestion that Jews must stay apart from these peoples or that they must be proselytized. Rather, what is envisaged is a process of coming together, a unification. The names of the gods and the worship of the gods will become united in the worship of Jehovah.

The interpretation I am suggesting is that God was over all nations. When people followed the truth as they knew it, God recognized that fact as meritorious. In every nation there were such people. Prophetically, it was proclaimed that there would be a time when these diverse peoples, with their various religions, would come together so that all who so served truth would serve the one God and would do so in His one name. To those who had knowledge of the God of Abraham, this truth had to be followed. There could be no turning away into other religions.

No claim can be made at this point that this interpretation has been proved. Nevertheless, the passages are intriguing and this interpretation is, at the least, not unreasonable. What is most interesting and important, however, is the evolving ideas in the Old Testament and that these same themes were taken up by Jesus and the Apostles. Through their teaching and practice, the ideas become clearer.

9

New Testament Documents

God shows no partiality.
—Peter

The New Testament is more specific in addressing the questions we are asking about cultural relativity and biblical religion. It portrays a religion which is to proselytize and "make disciples of all nations."[1] Jesus commanded his apostles to spread the message "in Jerusalem and in all Judea and Samaria and to the end of the earth."[2] Carrying out these orders, the early Christians were sure to encounter people from diverse cultures who held to different religions. At first, however, they not only did not obey Jesus' command, but there was active opposition to the first conversions of non-Jews when they occurred. The early Christians did not develop cross-cultural contacts easily. Yet, the New Testament does record the beginning process of communication with non-Jewish culture and within these accounts we can find answers to the questions we are raising.

The twenty-seven writings of the New Testament are reviewed in this chapter for the same purpose as was used in the previous chapter: to determine the consistency or inconsistency of these documents with what social science teaches about cultural relativity. This review is organized into three sections. The first, "The Gospels," covers the four biographies of Jesus (Matthew, Mark, Luke, and John). The second section, "The Early History," reviews the document of The Acts. The third, "Letters," discusses the letters written by the apostles to the early churches and church leaders. (The last Book in the New Testament, Revelation, is not relevant to the theme we are pursuing.)

The Gospels

Various sources in the biographies identified Jesus as having been both the Son of God and the King of Israel. Nathanael, for example, called him by both titles.[3] A man possessed by a demon called him the Son of the Most High God,[4] and a sign was placed by Pilate on the cross where Jesus was crucified that stated that he was the King of the Jews.[5] Jesus' interpretation to his disciples was that

106

his kingdom was "not of this world."[6] He never attempted to build an organization as such, but he consistently refused to limit his attention only to the Jewish nation.

Although Jesus once sent his apostles on a journey of ministry and charged them to go only among the Israelites, his objectives were never centered only within his own nation and culture.[7] The Gospel of John portrays Jesus as having been present and involved in the creation of "all things."[8] He was identified as a "light that enlightens every man."[9] Whatever interpretation is made of these references, they portray Jesus as oriented toward all nations and not only toward the Jews. This idea is made clear in his final statements to his apostles that, as the prophets had predicted, he would die and be resurrected. After this occurred, "repentance and forgiveness of sins should be preached in his name to all nations."[10] He later charged his followers in what is often called the Great Commission that they were to "make disciples of all nations."[11]

Jesus is portrayed as one who was faithful in Jewish worship but refused to participate in the ethnocentric customs of the Jews. He frequently surprised his friends and enraged others by seeking out non-Jews and regarding them also as people for whom God cared. His conversation with the Samaritan woman has been often noted. It was she who brought up the fact that the Jews had no dealings with the Samaritans.[12] He also healed the daughter of a Syrophenician woman who expressed the existence of the gulf between the Jews and the people of her own nation.[13] He taught by parable that it was a Samaritan who was the hero, while those who failed to show compassion were Jews.[14]

Jesus, however, went beyond these breaches of Jewish norms. He spoke approvingly of non-Jews while being critical of the Jews. So to the centurian, a non-Jew, he said:

> Truly, I say to you, not even in Israel have I found such faith. I tell you, many will come from east and west and sit at table with Abraham, Isaac, and Jacob in the kingdom of heaven, while the sons of the kingdom will be thrown into the outer darkness; there men will weep and gnash their teeth.[15]

On another occasion Jesus spoke to the Jews:

> Therefore I tell you, the kingdom of God will be taken away from you and given to a nation producing the fruits of it.[16]

These statements of Jesus indicate quite clearly that he did not participate in the narrow, ethnocentric perceptions current among his fellow Jews. It is also quite clear that he cared deeply about non-Jews, that he acknowledged that their faith could be genuine, and that he intended for his message to be spread among all the nations of the world. This by itself does not establish, however, that he would have accepted the interpretation that we can characterize as cultural relativity. But these statements are important in that they give us a sense of his approach—that he was a pluralist, at least in the sense that he cared about people whatever their ethnic and cultural background might be.

Absolutists give importance to the interpretation that the Christian message is absolute in the sense that salvation could only occur for those who accept Christ and become a participant in his church. There are four statements by Jesus that are considered to establish this view. The most often cited is one which will be considered later in detail. It seems to present a clear-cut statement: "I am the way, the truth, and the life; no one comes to the Father but by me."[17]

While this passage seems quite clearly to be absolutist, the other three passages often cited as being absolutist contain an important difference. In each case Jesus speaks not of those of other cultures, but those who know the message of Christ yet reject it.

> He who believes in him is not condemned; he who does not believe is condemned already, because he has not believed in the name of the only Son of God. And this is the judgment, that the light has come into the world, and men loved darkness rather than light, because their deeds were evil.[18]
>
> So everyone who acknowledges me before men, I also will acknowledge before my Father who is in heaven; but whoever denies me before men, I also will deny before my Father who is in heaven.[19]
>
> Everyone who comes to me and hears my words and does them, I will show you what he is like: he is like a man building a house, who dug deep, and laid the foundation upon rock. . . . But he who hears and does not do them is like a man who built a house on the ground without a foundation . . . [20]

Jesus, therefore, was quite explicit. The condemnation of the unbeliever was in the fact that he had rejected Jesus. He was not condemning the person who knew nothing about his teaching. Rather, he was passing judgment upon the individual whose knowledge was that Jesus' teaching was light, but who preferred darkness because of evil deeds and an unwillingness to reject evil. In this he spoke not of whether people favored him or opposed him but of a quality of character that sought or did not seek truth. He used this same point when he was examined by Pilate. Jesus' response was not to argue that he was the Son of God, but to emphasize the importance of seeking what is true. In his defense he stated:

> For this I have come into the world, to bear witness to the truth. Every one who is of the truth hears my voice.[21]

This was the same idea that he had taught earlier:

> If any man's will is to do his will, he shall know whether the teaching is from God or whether I am speaking on my own authority.[22]

The question as to why some people have faith and others do not is important. A basic concern of the absolutists is that cultural relativity is a pernicious idea that destroys faith. Jesus, however, was remarkable in his seeming lack of concern for the orthodoxy of interpretations. He emphasized that mistaken ideas were not so destructive as were wrong intentions. The question with the most priority was not whether a person believed Jesus was the Son of God, but whether or not a person wanted to follow light or darkness: would a person seek to know what was true and use what was true for the good?

What is still not clear is Jesus' evaluation of the person of another culture that had not heard the message of Christ in a meaningful way. On one occasion Jesus told a parable about servants whose master had gone away.[23] One servant realizing that the master would be away for an extended time began to beat the other servants and drink. But the master returned unexpectedly and condemned the servant. Jesus' interpretation was very explicit:

> And that servant who knew his master's will, but did not make ready or act according to his will, shall receive a severe beating. But he who did not know, and did what deserved a beating, shall receive a light beating. Every one to whom much is given, of him will much be required; and of him to whom men commit much they will demand the more.[24]

In this passage judgment is relative to knowledge but it is also relative to "light and truth." That is, the person who had knowledge and acted contrary to it was severely punished. But the behavior of the other servant who did not know the master's will but committed an act that by his own knowledge was an act of darkness was also punished though the punishment was less severe. Clearly, judgment was relative to both knowledge and will.

There are two other passages that give insight into Jesus' approach to this question. In the conversation with the Samaritan woman at the well, she brought up the question of the differences between the Samaritan and Jewish religions. Her question was therefore a "truth" question: Was it the true worship to worship in the mountain of Samaria or in the temple in Jerusalem? Jesus responded:

> The hour is coming when neither on this mountain nor in Jerusalem will you worship the Father. You worship what you do not know, we worship what we know, for salvation is from the Jews. But the hour is coming and now is, when the true worshipers will worship the Father in spirit and truth, for such the Father seeks to worship him. God is spirit, and those who worship him must worship in spirit and truth.[25]

Jesus refused to give her a simple answer to her question of whether it was one place or the other. Instead he contrasted the two religions, giving priority to that of the Jews as one that had been revealed. The nature of Samaritan religion, he stated, was that it lacked knowledge. Salvation was from the revelation of God and through the Jewish nation. Jesus was explicit about this. He did not, however, connect this with a judgment of lostness for all non-Jews. He spoke of a different approach to the worship of God that recognized that God was a spirit and worshiped in spirit and truth. Whatever exegesis is best for this scripture, the woman was not given an absolutist answer. Truth was again emphasized as important. It was clear that one could not reject what was believed to be true without condemnation. But no clear statement of the definition of truth was given. Instead, she—a human spirit—was told to worship the God spirit and to do so "in truth." Interestingly, she was not instructed to worship in Jerusalem.

There is yet one more statement in which Jesus seemed to provide a more simple and direct insight. This statement is much cited, yet its context seems to be too often ignored. It is the one passage in which Jesus spoke of his role as the judge of all nations. He specifically referred to a future time in which he would be upon a throne and would pronounce judgment upon all of the nations of the world:

> When the Son of man comes in his glory, and all the angels with him, then he will sit on his glorious throne. Before him will be gathered all the nations, and he will separate them one from another as a shepherd separates the sheep from the goats, and he will place the sheep at his right hand, but the goats at the left. Then the King will say to those at his right hand, "Come, O blessed of my Father, inherit the kingdom prepared for you from the foundation of the world; for I was hungry and you gave me food, I was thirsty and you gave me drink, I was a stranger and you welcomed me, I was naked and you clothed me, I was sick and you visited me, I was in prison and you came to me." Then the righteous will answer him, "Lord, when did we see thee hungry and feed thee, or thirsty and give thee drink? And when did we see thee a stranger and welcome thee, or naked and clothe thee? And when did we see thee sick or in prison and visit thee?" And the King will answer them, "Truly, I say to you, as you did it to one of the least of these my brethren, you did it to me." Then he will say to those at his left hand, "Depart from me, you cursed, into the eternal fire prepared for the devil and his angels; for I was hungry and you gave me no food, I was thirsty and you gave me no drink, I was a stranger and you did not welcome me, naked and you did not clothe me, sick and in prison and you did not visit me." Then they also will answer, "Lord, when did we see thee hungry or thirsty or a stranger or naked or sick or in prison, and did not minister to thee? Then he will answer them, "Truly, I say to you, as you did it not to one of the least of these, you did it not to me." And they will go away into eternal punishment, but the righteous into eternal life.[26]

In this passage Jesus interposed himself into the affairs of all nations. Some of the nations were to be rewarded by admission into a glorious land, but others would be sentenced to punishment. The criterion upon which the judgment would be made was explicitly stated: the extent to which each nation provided for the needy. As has already been noted, the context of this image is usually ignored. These words were not addressed to individuals but to nations. Jesus' judgment on the nations, whether it was approval or condemnation, was not based upon a doctrine such as whether one should worship on a mountain or in Jerusalem. It was based upon a standard that reflected Jesus' values and could be applied in all cultures. It could be equally applicable to Christian and non-Christian.

The passage portrays that all will be saved or lost on the basis of Jesus' judgment. Yet many of the saved did not know the "truth" on which they were being judged. Judgment involved Jesus even where Jesus was unknown, for Jesus took the part of the least people of a society. He was involved whether the people being judged knew it or not. Judgment was based upon the "golden rule" principle, a basic norm of Christian teaching. It is not a norm in non-Christian cultures. Yet in every culture, the treatment accorded the outcast is recognized as treatment to a fellow human.

We turn again to the main quotation of Jesus used by the absolutists: "I am the way, the truth, and the life; no one comes to the father but by me."[27] This passage, which may seem to be quite different from the picture of judgment already discussed, is not inconsistent with it. When Jesus explained his role in judgment, all were judged by him. He put himself into the role of the least people of society. Those who are approved and those who are condemned receive the judgment through him. This included the nations who had never heard of Jesus. They did not have to have knowledge of Jesus to be judged. In their treatment of the "least" people they were judged. It was not simply faith in Jesus that produced approval but faith that resulted in specific actions toward the "least" people. Similarly, nations which had no knowledge of Jesus could still treat the "least" in a way that produced salvation.

When interpretations such as I have suggested are made, there may be considerable opposition to them. This opposition usually focuses upon the contention that this kind of relativistic teaching will undermine the Christian faith and will destroy missionary efforts. After all, if non-Christians can be saved without Jesus, why should we send missionaries to them? My response to this also summarizes what I see as the basic concept of the minor prophets that was focused and expanded by Jesus. First, Jesus and the prophets consistently emphasized that the revelation of God was truth which enlightened and saved humans. Second, because this truth was valuable, there was an ongoing motivation for missionary work. Third, to say that Jesus judged nations on the basis of the treatment of the least was not to say that the nation did not need to know the love, forgiveness, and revelation which Jesus provided.

Jesus challenged the people of his day to break out of the ethnocentric attitudes that guided their thinking. This is no less important for us today. But is it not also evident that in doing this Jesus crossed cultural boundaries and provided values that work cross-culturally because he was beyond the ethnocentrism that was so prevalent?

There is nothing in the four accounts of Jesus' life that is inconsistent with what social scientists consider to be the theory of cultural relativity. Jesus' message, in fact, is amazing for its combination of the universal and the particular. Just as God's answer to Moses included both, so also Jesus' teaching emphasized both its applicability to all cultures and the specific importance of the Christian message. Jesus gave priority to the importance of loving truth over loving orthodoxy. He judged relative to knowledge and to the intention of the person. But he also set forth his own life and message as the specific revelation of God.

The Early History

The Book of Acts records the events of a rapidly growing church, whose early increase occurred because Jews were accepting the Christian faith. There were no efforts initially to convert non-Jews. Because of this, early growth did not involve issues of cross-cultural understanding. Christianity was rooted in the Jewish culture and whatever questions its acceptance raised for the Jews of that time, cross-cultural issues were not involved.

When the first non-Jew did become a Christian there was considerable controversy and, in fact, the controversy surfaced several times. In this process of moving Christianity from a sect of the Jews to an international and intercultural faith, the question of the relationship of this faith to other cultures was confronted, and from this we have some further insights into issues of cultural relativity and the Christian message.

The first non-Jew to become a Christian was Cornelius. He was an ideal person to break the barrier that the Jews maintained. The choice of Cornelius may be compared to the selection of Jackie Robinson as the first black man to break the segregation barrier of American baseball. Much has been written of the care in selecting Robinson because those who were managing the situation wanted a black man who would be able to stand the stress and be as acceptable as possible to racist whites. Any failures on the part of that first black man would be used as ammunition to oppose further integration.

Cornelius, as a Roman army officer, was a non-Jew but he was a "devout man who feared God, . . . gave alms liberally . . . and prayed constantly."[28] Stationed at Caesarea, he was about as much like a Jew as a non-Jew could be. Yet Peter at first rejected the idea of speaking to him about the Christian message. A vision and a voice from heaven were necessary to change Peter's mind, but when this happened Peter went to him and talked with him. After Cornelius became a Christian there was considerable controversy, and Peter was criticized.[29] Once the barrier was breached, however, other Christians were soon also taking the faith to non-Jews.[30] Undoubtedly, these non-Jews were not as devout or as close to Judaism as was Cornelius. But this was not necessary once non-Jews began to be accepted into the Christian faith. From that time on, the missionary work of the church included taking the Christian faith to people who did not have the cultural foundation of Judaism and therefore encountered Christianity across cultural boundaries.

When Peter initially spoke to Cornelius, part of what he said concerned his understanding of God's attitude toward non-Jews, "Truly I perceive that God shows no partiality, but in every nation any one who fears him and does what is right is acceptable to him."[31] Because these words were addressed to Cornelius who had faith in the Jewish God, they do not fully address the issues with which we are concerned. They do, however, clearly assert the principle that God has no partiality for one nation over another.

When Paul decided to devote his efforts to taking Christianity to the non-Jews, he moved directly into cross-cultural proselytism.[32] Two statements that he made are recorded in Acts and address the questions of relativism. At the Greek city of Lystra, he healed a crippled man and this convinced the people that both Paul and Barnabas were manifestations of their gods. They, of course, rejected this idea and spoke about Christ. Their speech contained the following words:

> In past generations [God] allowed all the nations to walk in their own ways; yet he did not leave himself without witness, for he did good and gave you from heaven rains and fruitful seasons, satisfying your hearts with food and gladness.[33]

In these words Paul explained that God had respected the integrity of the various cultures of the world. That is, he accepted that these people had various ways of living and dealing with the world around them, and he accepted them in their own right. He also asserted that the world itself was an evidence of a creator and sustainer and that represented a witness to God. The rain and crops that provided food and made them glad also were evidences of God. It seems obvious that this evidence could not have shown them any doctrines about this God. The non-Jew who lived in a village where there was no knowledge of even the existence of Jews was, however, said to have a witness to God in the productiveness of the natural environment. Such a person could appreciate this and attempt to express that appreciation in some form of worship. Such worship would be vastly different from the worship of the Jews under the law. But would it not be accepted by the God who shows no partiality and who allows such persons to continue in their own culture? That which we might want to call the religion of these people would be very non-Jewish—a "false" religion—but would be very acceptable to God.

It may be that we miss much of the significance of this passage because we have an adequate supply of food. We do not often give thought to "fruitful seasons." More troublesome still is the question of how a lack of food supply can destroy this witness to God. Thus there are areas of the world where hunger is prevalent and this witness may be destroyed. This passage seems to indicate that providing for the productivity of food and the elimination of hunger is more than an act of humanity. It is a part of the evidence of God.

Paul's second statement occurred when he was in Athens and addressed the men at the Areopagus. Paul began by expressing the perception that his listeners were "very religious."[34] Some interpreters have given a negative meaning to this phrase, but this is not textually accurate. Other interpreters have attempted to suggest a strategy on Paul's part that makes this statement insincere. These interpretations are unnecessary. Paul's statements about other faiths that we are considering indicate that his statement could very well have been sincere. Paul included the following words in his speech:

> [God] made from one every nation of men . . . that they should seek God, in the hope that they might feel after him and find him. Yet he is not far from each one of us. . . . The times of ignorance God overlooked but now he commands all men everywhere to repent, because he has fixed a day on which he will judge the world in righteousness by a man whom he has appointed, and of this he has given assurance to all men by raising him from the dead.[35]

This line of thought is similar to the one that we have already considered. Men did seek after God, but God was not distant: God was distant in the sense that many people had no contact with the Jewish faith. But God was not distant in the sense that the natural world was a witness to which all people could respond through worship as best they could conceptualize God. This would be to "seek God." Such seeking did involve "ignorance" in that there was no substantive revelation, but God "winked" at this. In his impartiality, God did not hold this against the non-Jew.

With the coming of the Christian faith, Paul contends in this passage, the message was to go out to all men and all were called upon to turn to this message. (The meaning of the word *repentance* is to turn.) Jesus was the center of this message and God would judge the righteousness of the world by him. The resurrection of Jesus was a signal that he was of God. This changed the teachings and responsibilities for those who knew the message. For them the full message—the doctrines and the commandments—were applicable. For those nations that did not know, their condition was unchanged.

There is one other passage that is often used to support the absolutist interpretation:

> And there is salvation in no one else, for there is no other name under heaven given among men by which we must be saved.[36]

Though sometimes used to support the idea that the native of a remote land without the Christian message is doomed, the context provides a very different interpretation. Peter spoke these words in Solomon's Portico of the temple of

Jerusalem. He was speaking to Jews and speaking to people who had the heritage of God's revelation through Abraham, Moses, and the Prophets. To these people, indeed, there was no one else by whom they could be saved. The evidence of Jesus was there, the revelation of God was there. If they rejected this truth, there was no other truth to save them. This in no way should suggest that the peasant in China who recognized the witness of the rain and the food and sought to be worshipfully thankful for this was not accepted by God. It is thus not contradictory to the ideas expressed in the other passages, nor is it inconsistent with the idea of cultural relativism.

To summarize, the evidence indicates that the early church was initially culture-bound. Christians spread the message among the Jews with whom they shared a common culture, but they resisted extending it to others. This resistance was broken when Peter extended the message to Cornelius, and soon non-Jews were converted into the Christian faith. The previous religion of these non-Jews was not evaluated as either true or false. What was asserted was that God's judgment was impartial, that the rain and harvests were evidences of God, and that people sought after God even though they did not have the knowledge of his revelation through the Jews. It was recognized as within God's will that these people continued to walk in their own ways. Yet it was also clear that the light of God's revelation was through Christ.

Letters

Paul, as the apostle to the non-Jews, traveled far from those areas where Jews were culturally dominant. Of his letters to the churches, the one to the Christians at Rome went the farthest geographically from the center of Judaism and Christianity in Jerusalem. In Rome, the capital of the empire, questions of pluralism, cross-cultural communication, and the truth of various religions would be most acute. And it was in the letter to Rome that Paul made some of the most explicit statements that relate to Christian absolutes and cultural relativity.

Very early in the letter, Paul wrote of his not being ashamed of the message of Christ because it was "the power of God for salvation to everyone who has faith, to the Jew first and also to the Greek." He continued the thought, pointing out that through faith there was life, but also that God's wrath was against "all ungodliness and wickedness of men who by their wickedness suppress the truth."[37] He then added a comment very similar to the one he told the people of Lystra:

> For what can be known about God is plain to them, because God has shown it to them. Ever since the creation of the world his invisible nature, namely, his eternal power and deity, has been clearly perceived in the things that have been made. So they are without excuse. For although they

knew God they did not honor him as God or give thanks to him, but they became futile in their thinking and their senseless minds were darkened.[38]

Paul's words again take the position that for Jew and non-Jew alike, the world was itself a testimony to the existence of a power. When people refused to follow the implications of this—refused to honor this creation—they suppressed truth, and this was without excuse. The preaching of the Gospel, with its explicit revelation of God's message, was an antidote for such failure. It created faith that saved. It is important to note that the condemnation made in the passage was directed toward those who suppressed what truth they had. It was not directed toward the Chinese peasant who had responded to whatever concept of truth was available to him.

Just a little further in the letter Paul expanded his comments on this:

> When Gentiles who have not the law do by nature what the law requires they are a law to themselves, even though they do not have the law. They show that what the law requires is written on their hearts, while their conscience also bears witness and their conflicting thoughts accuse or perhaps excuse them on that day when, according to my gospel, God judges the secrets of men by Christ Jesus.[39]

A basic answer to the questions has now taken shape. Non-Jews without God's explicit revelation in the Mosaic Law were not to be judged according to a law they did not have. But the basic thrust of that revealed law, though unknown to them, was not that distinct from what they knew. Jesus summarized the law and the prophets into two commandments: a thorough love of God and to love one's neighbor as oneself.[40] The peasant in China could have known the power of the creation, been thankful for the rain and harvests, responded to these and loved his neighbor. These might have been expressed through Confucianism, Taoism, or some folk religion. This would have been the basis upon which he would have been judged even as the nation in which he lived was judged on the basis of its provision for the least of their people.[41] The judgment thus was neither arbitrary nor was it partial. It was based upon general principles central to the Judeo-Christian culture. It expressed the cultural criteria of the Bible, yet it did so in a way that made it applicable in all cultures.

Paul again comments:

> Or is God the God of Jews only? Is he not the God of Gentiles also? Yes, of Gentiles also, since God is one; and he will justify the circumcised on the ground of their faith and the uncircumcised through their faith.[42]

The sign of the Jewish faith was circumcision. The non-Jew had neither the sign nor the faith. But as there is only one God, Paul contended, that one God was concerned with both Jews and non-Jews. He judged the non-Jews on the basis of "their faith"—their non-Jewish, non-Christian faith—not one that was unknown to them.

There are other passages in these letters that do not speak to the issue in this same way, but they do indicate that God's judgment was relative to the situation, knowledge, and culture of the individual. One of these was the statement from James, "Whoever knows what is right to do and fails to do it, for him it is sin.[43] Does this not reasonably suggest that, at least for some behaviors, it is the understanding a person has that determines whether God judges it to be sin and not just the doing of a particular behavior itself? This idea was made quite clear when Paul wrote to the Romans about a number of points of disagreement they were having. His statement was, "Let everyone be fully convinced in his own mind."[44] Concerning whether it was right to eat meat that had been offered to idols, he added to illustrate the general principle: "But he who has doubts is condemned, if he eats, because he does not act from faith; for whatever does not proceed from faith is sin."[45]

Judgment thus was to be based upon the intentions of the person acting. The act must be constructive. If the individual acted with the understanding that it was true and good, it was not sin. However, if the person thought that it might not be right and true but did it anyway—it was sin. Paul's statement in this same passage that "nothing is unclean in itself" seems to suggest that in many decisions, the reason why we choose as we do is crucial.[46] These passages establish that it was also within a particular culture that behavior was considered to be relative to the individual's understanding of it.

Five remaining biblical statements might seem to offer support for the absolutist interpretation. The first has often been used in this way, "For no other foundation can any one lay than that which is laid, which is Jesus Christ."[47] The interpretation that has emerged in this book has no difficulty with this statement. What has been contended is that Jesus' teaching as he expressed it, and as taught by the apostles, did not turn this one statement into an absolute by which the whole world would be judged by its affiliation (or lack of affiliation) with the Christian religion. It is important to note that this passage was written to a church—the one at Corinth—to build and strengthen it. Most certainly the church can have no other foundation. That does not mean that other religions and institutions do not have other foundations. It does not cancel the idea expressed in the other passages that God is also concerned for the Chinese peasant who responds in his own culture and religion to that which he can know of God. It does not cancel the biblical statement that the Chinese peasant will be judged according to his faith.[48]

The second passage has a different emphasis:

> What do I imply then? That food offered to idols is anything or that an idol is anything? No, I imply that what pagans sacrifice they offer to demons and not to God.[49]

If idols are demons, the offering of sacrifices would seem to constitute something other than the worship of people seeking God but without knowledge of
his revelation. If our concept of a demon is a being of Satan, idols were not
demons. Idols were the lifeless creations of human hands. But the Greek
meaning of demon was that it was an inferior divine being. And Paul, writing to
a Greek city, would have been likely to use the word in the sense of its meaning
to Greeks. In its context, it is clear that idols of themselves are neither gods nor
devils. But just as Paul, when addressing the Greeks in Athens, considered their
gods to be evidence of religious commitment, so also the offering of sacrifices to
idols by the Corinthians was considered as evidence of commitment. Paul's point
was that this religious commitment was to an inferior object.

The third passage is concerned with the intimate bond of marriage:

> Do not be mismated with unbelievers. For what partnership have righ-
> teousness and iniquity? Or what fellowship has light with darkness? What
> accord has Christ with Belial? Or what has a believer in common with an
> unbeliever? What agreement has the temple of God with idols?[50]

Here the distinction between the Christian and non-Christian is most explicit. But a commandment appropriate for the marriage relationship may not be
applicable to other situations. A married couple lives within the same culture
and is exposed to the same ideas. The unbeliever in Corinth married to a
Christian would have known and have rejected the Christian faith. This was
altogether a different situation from that of the Chinese peasant who knew
nothing of Christianity.

In the fourth passage, Paul writes that Jesus' judgment inflicts "vengeance
upon those who do not know God and upon those who do not obey the gospel of
our Lord Jesus."[51] This statement is made to the Thessalonians about those who
were persecuting them:

> This is evidence of the righteous judgment of God, that you may be made
> worthy of the kingdom of God for which you are suffering—since indeed
> God deems it just to repay with affliction those who afflict you.[52]

Those persecuting the Thessalonians had had exposure to the message of the
Christian faith. They evidently preferred darkness to light. That they did not
know God was not because the knowledge was unavailable. Again, they were
quite different people in a different situation from that of the peasant in China.

The last passage to be considered is in a letter from Peter:

> But by the same word the heavens and earth that now exist have been
> stored up for fire, being kept until the day of judgment and destruction of
> ungodly men.[53]

An important point of interpretation is the definition of "ungodly men." Did it include the Chinese peasant no matter what the character of his life? Or did it refer to those who rejected that which they could have known of God? In this passage the specific reference is to "scoffers" who follow "their own passions."[54] The reference is clearly to ungodly men who knew of God but rejected him.

In the next chapter, the various interpretations will be tied together. At this point, a reminder may be helpful—the purpose here has been to review each passage that seemed to have relevance to the issue of Christian absolutes and cultural relativity in order to make some observations of the nature of biblical teaching.

When I began this study there were a few passages which seemed to indicate that the teaching of the Bible might not be as absolutist as it has usually been interpreted. In determining to read the Bible specifically with this issue in mind, I was not prepared for what I discovered. Upon completion of this reading, it seemed quite evident to me that the Bible presented an explicit and systematic interpretation of this issue that is consistent with cultural relativity but quite inconsistent with the traditional representations of absolutists.

Such a discovery necessarily raised an insistent question: why had I never noticed these teachings before? The answer that I reached is very mundane. Previously I had read into the passages the orthodox meanings that had been taught to me as being "the Christian faith," and I had not previously asked the question with the mindset of a student.

10

An Interpretation of the Review

The best part of our knowledge is that which teaches where
knowledge leaves off and ignorance begins.

—O. W. Holmes

Three questions have emerged that summarize the issue as to whether the Bible is absolutist or relativist. The first concerned whether the nature of revelation taught in the Bible fits better the view held by absolutists or relativists. The second question asked what the Bible taught about persons of other religions. The third question evaluated whether there was evidence that biblical evaluations were made relative to the culture and knowledge of individuals. From the answers gained to these questions could come insights for the question of relativity. The answers to all three questions supported the view that the biblical text is fully consistent with those of cultural relativity but not with absolutism.

This conclusion contradicts the expectations of both absolutists and relativists. Absolutists have asserted that for knowledge to be reliable, it must be absolute. They have believed the Bible to be absolutist and have been successful in portraying it as such through an emphasis on selected texts. Sociologists have assumed that orthodox Christian believers must also be absolutists. Similarly, they have also assumed that the Bible—the Book of the fundamentalists—must be absolutist.

Absolutists continue to contend that religious beliefs other than those in the Bible are untrue and those who believe them are lost. Typical of this is the Christian school principal who said, "We negate all the other religions of the world. . . . They're wrong. There is no way of getting into heaven except through Jesus Christ."[1] For these people it is considered heresy to speak of non-Christians being approved by God, of other religious systems as being in any sense acceptable to God, or of non-Christians who worship another deity being acknowledged by God as worshiping God. Yet all three views are biblical teachings.

The following summarizes the answers derived from this examination of the biblical text. First, the events of the nineteen centuries from Abraham to Jesus are consistent with the culturally relative processes by which knowledge is defined within a culture. That is, if all human truth is relative and requires a cultural setting to confirm it, any revelation from God would become relative the moment it was expressed in human language and communicated to humans. As such it also would require a group of people participating in a culture to give it the authenticity of truth. The record of the Old Testament is that of just such a cultural process—of a "people of God"—through which the revelation was mediated.

To develop a culture that would grow out of a revelation from God would require a long period of development. The call to Abraham, the development of a "nation of slaves in Egypt," the exodus, the true nationhood, and the exile and return were all momentous events in this process from the initial implementation of the plan to the fulfilling of the promise in the ministry of Christ. The theory of cultural relativity that sees all knowledge as dependent upon a social group to give it authenticity is fully consistent with the record of God's dealings with the Israelites. The culture that emerged first in Jewish and then Christian groups provided a vehicle for authenticating the truth of its message.

What is sometimes portrayed as the "Old Testament warrior God" as compared to the "New Testament God of love" can be understood better in terms of the need of cultural processes. The "warrior" idea stems from the interpretation that God commanded the Jews to exterminate all non-Jews in their area of settlement. This commandment, it is important to note, was directed toward any who worshiped other Gods—both Jews and non-Jews—and was limited to that particular period of time. It was geared to establishing the Israelites as a nation distinct from other peoples. It was not a feature of the "Old Testament God" but of a particular stage in the cultural development of Israel. It was necessary for the establishment of a new society with its distinctive culture that they isolate themselves from other peoples. Indeed, their failure to carry out this commandment was harmful to the nation for several centuries. If their culture was to develop, it had to take place in a location, and this required a degree of isolation from other cultural influences. Realistically, it is difficult to understand how else it could have been obtained. The biblical text repeatedly makes evident that the "Old Testament God" like the "New Testament God" was compassionate, patient, and concerned with all nations.

The long development of Judaism was precisely that which would have been required—according to our current knowledge of processes of cultural development and relativity—if the message of God were to be revealed. If revelation were absolute, why would the nations of the world be left in ignorance through all the centuries during which the Jewish culture was being developed? The biblical record of events from the time of God's promise to Abraham to its fulfillment in Christ is consistent with a world of cultural relativity.

To answer the second question, biblical truth was given as the truth of events, not ideas. God's self-description to Moses was, "I am the God of Abraham,

Isaac, and Jacob." What proof was this that there was a God? The proof was to be found in the God who was known through the events in the lives of Abraham, Isaac, and Jacob. God would later also be known by the events that brought Israel out of bondage in Egypt to freedom. These were not assertions of absolutes, but the acts of God, through which his message was introduced into the world. An act is simply an event that occurred at a particular time and place. It is neither absolute nor relative. But the human understanding of these events—because it is human—is always relative.

The biblical writers repeatedly made reference to various deities without feeling the need to identify them as false. It was only in the late prophetic period that clear statements were made that the idols worshiped by the peoples were "no-gods." When Christianity began to be taught to the people of other nations, an interpretation toward the other nations was made explicit. People who did not know God were to be judged according to how they responded to that which they did know—thankfulness for what they had, the way they followed the god they knew, and the way they treated the least people in their society. God showed no partiality to people simply because by birth accident they happened to be where they could know the biblical message.

The answer to the third question is that biblical teaching accepted the relative nature of human knowledge. Standards of judgment for those who did not know about God's revelation were given. These standards may or may not lead to condemnation and are relative to the knowledge of the people. Clearly, people were not condemned for not knowing what they could not have known. Other passages were found that stated that among Christians, judgment also would be relative to both the knowledge and intentions of the individual. This biblical acceptance of relativity does not compromise the point of view that God is truth and God's revelations are true.

Both the Jews and the early Christians wanted to limit God's work to their own definition of it. Perhaps this is a tendency for all of us. Paul Tillich's concept of a "God who is beyond God" may be helpful here. He referred to the fact that God is always greater and more comprehensive than the human understanding of him. The reality of God is always beyond our greatest idea of him. Yet our knowledge is always held and expressed as human knowledge. Though cultural relativity can contribute nothing about the reality of God, it does help us to understand the nature and limitations of our understanding of God. The danger of absolutism is that it is inaccurate in its understanding of human knowledge. In this, it also leads to ethnocentric distortions of biblical teaching. The biblical approach was to call the Jews, and later the people of all nations, not by condemnation of their religious views as false and meaningless, but to join in the God who was greater than all of their ideas of God.

Jesus often moved beyond the narrow precepts of Jewish culture and recognized faithfulness among non-Jews. He put into practice the idea that God was the God of all nations. He was concerned about the well-being of people, including their spiritual relationships. He was never one to promote only a narrow spirit but could speak with people such as the Samaritan woman in a way that would address her needs and direct her spiritual life without what we would today call "hard-sell proselytism." He was concerned for her "thirst," not for attacking the errors of Samaritan religion. His image of judging the nations was based not upon a particular doctrine but upon how each nation treated the least of its citizens. There is in all of this a recognition of the religion of others and an invitation to them to grow in their understanding of God.

The Apostles were involved in several controversies that had as their basis the questions of pluralism. One party held that Gentiles had to become Jews before becoming Christians. The view prevailed, however, that this type of nationalistic, sectarian approach was not appropriate, and that Christianity was more inclusive. To the Greek philosophers, Paul preached not a message of condemnation but one that drew upon their culture, and introduced the message of Christ. In his writings, Paul speaks of those who did not have the law of God as being judged according to their own consciences and their own religions. That is, they were judged according to adherence to that which they knew to be true and good.

Indeed, the basic way by which people find the truth, according to the Bible, is through a desire to know truth. The basic way by which the practice of truth is judged is by the treatment given to the "least" people. God's truth was said to be available to all—not in the explicit revelation of which many had no knowledge—but in the created world, the rain, and the harvest of food. It is in the way that people respond to these that they recognize God or fail to do so. Clearly such people did not know the doctrines of the Christian faith. Unfortunately, these biblical teachings are not given emphasis in conventional absolutist expressions. It is for this reason that they seem unusual and questionable.

These ideas are troublesome for absolutists. They seem to be what Christian liberalism and universalism have contended for many years, that God will save non-Christians and that essentially one can know God through any religion. Therefore, according to the absolutists, to accept these ideas even in a most limited way puts one on the slippery slope to atheism and destroys all missionary and evangelistic motivation. Any hint of support for this concept leaves one open to attack. The popular evangelical speaker, Tony Campolo, experienced this when his speech to a national convention was cancelled and he was subjected to extensive cross-examination in print as to his orthodoxy. Absolutist assumptions were the standard, and Campolo was charged with universalism mainly because of his use of Matthew 25. The account of this episode is not reassuring that an attempt to understand the biblical teaching or to directly consider his interpretation took place.[2]

If a non-Christian can be saved, the following question is invariable raised: "What does a Hindu or Muslim gain by becoming a Christian?" Nothing it seems, that he really did not have before.[3] This question is exactly the same as

Provision for a purpose

fulfill men rests in the fulfillment

God's

that which Paul knew the Roman Christians would have upon reading in his letter that God could approve and accept people who did not have God's word.[4] He posed the question for them, "Then what advantage has the Jew?" Paul then answers his question and in doing this answers the objection that absolutists pose: "Much in every way. To begin with the Jews were entrusted with the oracles of God."[5] So also, the advantage of the Christian is the knowledge of the oracles. That is, Christians have the message of God. The Bible calls this a light to our pathways through life. It conveys to us the grace of God. We have understanding. Without it, we would be groping in darkness. No wonder Paul says that the advantage of having the word of God was "Much in every way"!

That absolutists will be concerned about the interpretation made here is understandable, but there is also a disturbing facet to their concern. Does the message of Christ mean so little that unless it is absolutely necessary for salvation, there is no real reason to have it? It is interesting to note what Paul wrote to Galatian Christians who had come from non-Jewish backgrounds:

> Formerly, when you did not know God, you were in bondage to beings that by nature are no gods; but now that you have come to know God, or rather to be known by God, how can you turn back again to the weak and beggarly elemental spirits, whose slaves you want to be once more?[6]

Paul similarly emphasizes the importance of Christianity in his letter to the Christians at Thessalonica:

> For they themselves report concerning us what a welcome we had among you, and how you turned to God from idols, to serve a living and true God.[7]

Peter also wrote: *fulfillment rest in the vindication of God's purpose*

> But you are a chosen race, a royal priesthood, a holy nation, God's own people, that you may declare the wonderful deeds of him who called you out of darkness into his marvelous light.[8]

The authors did not condemn as lost those who followed whatever knowledge they had. But neither did they consider evangelism a matter of indifference. They regarded the non-Jews who were now Christians as having come from darkness to light, from bondage to freedom, and from serving lifeless idols to the living God. Clearly they considered knowledge of God and his work better than ignorance, even though people could know something of God by the world and respond to it in their ignorance.

Absolutists may decry this interpretation as universalism. My response would be: what do these biblical passages that have been discussed in the last three chapters mean? The attacks on Tony Compalo and similar statements do not focus upon Biblical teaching, but upon absolutist orthodoxy. I hope the difference between what I am advocating and the notion that "one religion is as good as another" is clear. The Bible rejects this notion, but it also rejects the absolutist assumptions.

Perhaps because of the past attacks upon traditional Christian beliefs, there is a defensive resistance to these ideas. This is understandable. To speak approvingly of non-Christian religion seems to many people to lessen the ultimacy of the Christian faith.

But the opposite case needs to be considered: absolutist assertions compromise the standards of the Christian faith. Individuals raised in Christian homes, Christian churches, and communities where the Christian message is available can become believers simply by conforming to their social environments. Those born into families and communities where the Christian message was either unknown or opposed are in a very different situation. They are unlikely to become Christians. Traditional absolutist interpretations carefully separate the believers as approved from the unbelievers who are the condemned. They ignore the teaching of Jesus that those who know the message of God will be judged by a different standard than will the persons who do not know the message.[9] Absolutist designations of the saved and the lost insist on an absolute standard of judgment—that of being a Christian. This may be reassuring to the Christian, but it severely compromises the biblical message. It may contribute to the self-righteousness and condemnatory attitude often in evidence among Christians.

It is easier to be judged according to whether we have faith in Christ than whether we practice the "golden rule" of providing for the least people in our society.[10] Judged by the standard of being a believer in Christ, I can be confident. After all, I am not an atheist, Buddhist or Muslim. But the standard of judgment Jesus used provides a different basis for judgment—one that is too often unmentioned. The absolutist assertions have a way of making us self-satisfied and less likely to pay attention to the biblical standards of the Christian life. The thesis put forward here inevitably calls into question the complacency arising from the belief that because we have a commitment of faith in Christ we are saved, and those who do not are inevitably lost.

The revelation of God as presented in the Bible was both a revelation and the development of a culture among people who would subsequently support and sustain the knowledge of this revelation. Within this culture, social interaction would sustain the revelation as real and true. It is important to remember that this need for a culture to define truth is a characteristic of all knowledge systems and not just religion or Christianity. The people who participated in this culture would be human and their social processes human—thus relative. It was to provide a culture to sustain the revelation that God developed the Jewish nation. The life of Christ led to the emergence of Christian culture that refers to the culture of Christians who provided the social base for sustaining the truth of God's revelation after Jesus.

It is crucial not to confuse this concept of Christian culture with Christendom, though the terms have been used as synonyms. Christendom refers to those periods when the church so dominated society and the political power of nations that the whole realm was referred to as Christian. This is one definition of Christian culture, but it is not the meaning I am using. The eras when the church had such social power were also eras when the church created the grossest of injustices.

Christian culture, as I use the term, refers to that culture shared among people that is directly derived from the teachings of Jesus as distinct from a culture that develops in society. The church inevitably intermingles cultural elements of its society with those of its biblical origins, yet the origins remain and can be utilized as the standard for the Christian faith.

To those within the Christian culture, beliefs and norms have been established even as they are in any viable culture. A member cannot do anything he or she wishes to do. Christian culture is not chaos but a system of truth with beliefs and norms for behavior. It is often observed that converts in foreign missionary programs have difficulty relinquishing their cultural traits for those of Christianity. What we tend to miss is that this is no different from that which Christians experience in our own culture. If we fail to notice the discrepancy between being a good citizen of our communities and nation and being a Christian, it is an indication that we have the same difficulty. Christian culture and the culture of a nation are inevitably different. The Christian must be a citizen of two worlds. Cultural relativism does not negate the beliefs or norms of the Christian culture. It will, however, help us to separate the elements of the two worlds that so easily get intertwined in our understanding.

The beginning of attempts to integrate Christianity and scientific thinking has often been dated back to the work of Frederich Schliermacher, who attempted to make Christianity creditable to the secular intellectual world. Its standards of truth were those of his contemporary culture. Basically, these interpretations were attempts to start with the prevailing secular culture and make the religious system appealing to it. Fundamentalism emerged as a resistence to these syncretistic attempts and has remained very wary of such efforts; this is understandable. But it also makes it important to reiterate that the thesis here is very different from either the Schliermacher type of liberalism or the fundamentalist absolutism. My contention is that the Christian religion represents a culture that developed with its own criteria of truth, originating in the call of Abraham. This culture has continued to exist in interaction with other cultures. Sometimes it has accommodated, sometimes it has opposed, and sometimes it has isolated itself. Christianity in its documents and in its traditions has asserted its claim to truth. It proclaims its truths to be light as opposed to darkness including the darkness of other religions and philosophies.

But the Bible makes such claims in a way that is consistent with the insights of cultural relativity. That is, the Bible makes its claims without the narrowness of absolutism which derogates alternatives. It is able, therefore, to deal with the relative definitions of truth encountered in various societies. Its claims are based in events rather than absolute dogma. Its doctrines are derived from those events.

Far from being detrimental to Christianity, an understanding of cultural relativity is immensely helpful in understanding and communicating the message. It takes seriously the development of the Judeo-Christian culture as a historical event in its own right. It recognizes the importance of the church— the congregation—in preserving the authenticity of a Christian culture. It provides an understanding of cultural processes through which Christian truth and the contemporary culture of the world can be separated. And it provides insights for more effectively communicating the Christian message to other cultures. It does nothing to undercut the Christian's faith in the truth of God's revelation, though it provides insights into the complexity of the process of that revelation.

Part IV
Negotiations

11

Can a "Believer" Accept Cultural Relativity?

> I was beginning to see that there were in modern times a number
> of people of sharp perceptions and keen wit who actually did believe
> Christianity, not in any softened, modernized version, but in all the
> roughness and strangeness of its ancient form.
>
> —Emilie Griffin

In this section, "Negotiations" does not use its primary meaning but its colloquial definition. In its primary definition, it refers to the action when two persons or groups attempt to come to an agreement. Usually such agreements are not exactly what either party would wish, but through compromise an agreement is reached. But I want to be very explicit: there is no contention here that absolutists and relativists should compromise their respective viewpoints to accommodate each other. Absolutists are committed to a religious faith and have no reason to compromise it for the sake of agreement. Similarly, social scientists and secular humanists are committed to a basic method of studying human behavior. The integrity of each should preclude compromise.

The colloquial use of the term, however, refers to the effort "to successfully travel along or over, to complete, to accomplish." This would be the meaning of the term when someone is said to have negotiated a car down a highway with snowdrifts. The individual has reached the destination without becoming snowbound. It may not have been easily achieved, but there has been no compromise of objective. The negotiations in this section are intended to consider whether Christians can accomplish the objectives of the faith without compromise and also accept cultural relativity. In the next chapter the further issue of the possible advantages in doing this will be considered. After that the same issues will be considered from the opposite direction—that is, for the social scientist.

This is, in different words, the question about "the wall" introduced in the first chapter. This mental wall between absolutists and relativists has isolated these two categories of people from each other, so that the two sides have been considered irreconcilable opposites. But is the wall necessary? Can a Christian believe in the Bible as God's revelation and still negotiate through the social sciences without compromise?

The answer to these questions, as has already been made evident, is affirmative. Absolutism is not a necessary part of Christianity. A Christian can accept the Bible as fully God's word and without compromise also accept cultural relativity. But to do this will require a considerable rethinking of biblical teaching. For those who have been socialized into Christianity with an absolutist approach, they have been conditioned to interpret certain passages in a particular direction and to ignore the impact of other passages. It is not easy to change one's customary way of thinking.

Any change in a basic view is unsettling. One writer has expressed the feeling in the following way: "It was as if the ground had been pulled out from under one, with no firm foundation to be seen anywhere upon which one could have built."[1] These words may seem to fit the experience of an absolutist Christian who has become aware of comparative cultures and the relativity of human knowledge. Actually, they were written by Albert Einstein about the upheavals in physics in the 1920s. To have one's view of the world disturbed is necessarily upsetting, and it is understandable that some will avoid it at all cost. But fear that keeps us from perceiving may ultimately prove to be harmful.

Christian believers who accept cultural relativity must reorient their thinking away from absolutist pronouncements. The new orientation is basically to be discovered in the realization that Christianity itself is a culture. It exists within various societies and is influenced by these cultures yet it retains in itself a set of values, beliefs, and norms that are distinct. As such it is subject to all of the processes of culture. Yet it also has aspects about it that are distinguishing. It is not, for example, the culture of any one society. It is not the culture of Christendom. It draws upon the Bible as a special source of self-definition and refers to the culture that directly developed from these origins.

This culture is traced back to Abraham, who was called to withdraw from the culture in which he lived to create a new nation with a culture originating in God's call. The result of this new culture was the nation of Israel. It was within this nation that Jesus appeared to be what sociologists would call a cultural innovator. His work was portrayed in the New Testament as clearly within and building upon this cultural heritage. He interpreted his own work as being to "fulfill the law."[2] This culture has continued into our current age. It has picked up and abandoned traits, as all living cultures do. It exists today as a cultural alternative to other lifestyles, national cultures, political ideologies, hedonism, or whatever people seek to find meaning in their lives and existence.

Where then, in this scheme of things, do the absolutists fit in? The potential for absolutism exists in all cultures. It grows out of the logic of experience. That is, any person successfully socialized into any culture will feel that the beliefs of that culture are self-evidently true. Similarly, conflicting beliefs will seem inadequate and obviously wrong. This surety will be very convincing. There is nothing unusual about this aspect of absolutism. In fact, part of Jesus' teaching was to break down the absolutes of his followers. It was to break them out of the mold of thinking that held that God was concerned more with their own nation than the people of other nations. They were to relinquish the notion that they alone were God's workers.[3]

In fact, absolutist thinking may be the result of a vital culture. Cultures that are dying do not generate absolutism because they become incapable of being successfully internalized into the personalities of their adherents. It is a sign of the vitality and success of a culture when the temptation to absolutist thinking exists. But absolutism also tends to develop rigidity that interferes with functioning. It may become a defense against internal doubt. In such a situation, it is not a sign of vitality but a declining belief system.

Absolutism also can be culturally transmitted. When it is a part of the belief structure—the culture—it will be explicitly taught. In this situation, absolutism represents neither a vital belief system nor one that is declining. Rather, it is a component of the teaching of the faith. A result of the controversies of the recent past has been that defenders of the Christian faith have evolved into a position where absolutist thinking has been seen as necessary in defense of the faith. They have taught this and their students have learned it and had their thought systems, in turn, shaped by it. Thus, those who have learned absolutism well have become extremely sensitive to the idea that any breach of the wall with cultural relativity would ultimately destroy their faith. Christians who have not been so taught may not have this sensitivity. Many Christians are defenders of absolutism today because that is the way they have been taught—not because it is a biblical doctrine. But to have learned the lesson well means that it will be difficult to accept the idea that the Bible is not absolutist.

All three characteristics seem evident among Christian absolutists. For some it is vitality. Their faith and experiences as Christians are such that they cannot imagine other cultures where people think otherwise. For others it is defensiveness. Lurking in their conscious or unconscious thoughts are fears that their faith may not be ultimately true, and they carefully guard against facing this terror. For still others, it is a consequence of having been taught that Christianity is absolutist.

If the interpretation of the Bible given here is accurate, the fact is clear that the Bible does not base its teaching on absolutes at all but on events. These events happened at a particular time and place. Events are never absolute or relative, they simply occur. Other religions have other approaches. The acceptance of Buddhism is grounded in a certain world view which is experienced as being "enlightened." Islam asserts its absolutism in many ways including its basic statement: "There is no got but Allah."

But, contrary to these, the Bible only asserts certain events and the meaning of these events. God is not presented as an absolute truth—sometimes not even as the only deity. Rather, he is the God of Abraham, Isaac, and Jacob. He is the

God who led the Israelites out of Egypt. He is the God who sent his son, Jesus, to live among us. He is the God of events. When asked to explain himself, this was the way he wanted to be identified in all ages.

This heritage is portrayed in the eleventh chapter of Hebrews, where a series of persons who lived across the centuries were cited for their faith. "By faith, Abraham obeyed. . . ," "By faith Sarah conceived. . . ," "By faith Moses . . . was hid. . . ," and so the chapter continues, a recitation of events. This is the foundation of the Christian religion: events not absolutes. The cumulative record of these events make up a "cloud of witnesses" for those who are alive and living within this culture.[4] It is the calling of the Christian to continue this culture and add new events of faith to the record.

Where then is the challenge in cultural relativity? It is not there. If God spoke, he spoke. The fact that the world is one in which human knowledge is characterized by cultural relativity in no way prevents revelation. Only when we ignore the Christian faith as being a record of events and make it into absolutist doctrines do we fall into a situation where cultural relativism becomes a threat. Other religions and political ideologies are vulnerable when they are grounded in absolutist assertions. Communism, for example, is dependent upon a form of economic class determinism. Without this absolute, the ideology is without foundation. But Christianity is not like that, because it is grounded in events.

This is not to say that there is no problem. In fact, it shifts us to a different problem. If Christianity is grounded in events, how do we know whether these events really occurred? This question has been pursued in the past through extensive efforts to get at the historical question and find the "historical Jesus." For a religion of events, the accuracy of the history would seem to be crucial. Did Moses really live and lead the Israelites through the Red Sea? Did Jesus really rise and live after being executed on the cross? The answer is, of course, that we do not really know in the sense of possessing decisive historical proof. There is a written record in the Bible that says these things happened. But there are other written records that claim that other things happened that we do not believe. It is usually considered obvious that not everything that has been written really happened. In our current scientific age where events are often recorded not only in writing but on videotape, the historicity of ancient events—especially if they portray miraculous events that we have not witnessed—seems impossible.

But it is just at this point in which the study of culture, including that of cultural relativity, becomes helpful. We cannot prove an event that happened in the distant past. (In fact, most events in the recent past could not be proved.) We, therefore, cannot prove that Jesus came back to life after he was killed. What cannot be denied, however, is that there developed a cultural belief among a large number of people that he did. Our knowledge of culture can tell us that something happened. Such a society does not develop out of the imagination alone. It happens around events of some sort that become incorporated into the ongoing life of people. What is undeniable is that this cultural phenomenon—

Christianity—is still with us, and its self-explanation is in the record of events in the Bible.

This biblical record and Christian culture present themselves to us as an interpretation of the world, its meaning, and how one ought to live. Every individual, whether by conscious search or unconscious accommodation, decides by what view of reality and meaning that person lives. To refuse to make the decision, or to say that such a decision is impossible, is simply to accede to whatever general view is prevalent. This would be no less a decision. There are competing cultures and subcultures—competing views of reality and meaning—from which we make the decisions of our lives. But we cannot avoid the choice. The most difficult obstacle to Christian faith stems from the power of the contemporary scientific, technological, and materialistic society. Indeed it seems so powerful we may be persuaded to discount what is old and foreign. But it is precisely this power that cultural relativity undermines. For it can destroy this chronocentrism that sees the present as inevitably superior to the past. Once we begin to be free from this, we can examine all events and beliefs for possible truth—not just those that are contemporary.

Once free from the hold of chronocentrism, the biblical question can be faced: "What do you think of the Christ?"[5] We then must determine whether the culture derived from the biblical events represents a superior culture to competing views. We cannot deny its historical existence or origin. It is from this basis that we can choose. When the issue is posed in this manner, cultural relativity—far from being an enemy—has clearly become an aid. It has undercut our ethnocentric and chronocentric propensities. Furthermore, we are now asking the question in a manner that makes sense to the contemporary consciousness.

We have established a common ground with secular humanists, relativists, and others, so that the presentation of the Christian faith becomes possible for meaningful consideration. The Christian has negotiated the path without needing to wall out social science. The feared consequences of cultural relativity have vanished.

12

The Contributions of Cultural Relativism for Christian Belief

> You have taught me to worship a god who is like you, who shares
> your thinking exactly.
>
> —Garrison Keillor

Having concluded that Christians can negotiate their objectives without walling out cultural relativism, we turn to the question of the potential value in doing so. To say that it is valuable does not mean that it is necessary. Christians can certainly live faithful and meaningful lives without ever knowing of the term "cultural relativism" or the contributions it presumably might provide. But because we live in what is increasingly a "small world" or "global village" where the impact of the pluralism is increasing, it is likely that there will be a continuing increase in that segment of the population that encounters competing belief systems. Pluralism produces a sense of cultural relativism even when people are uninformed on the issues of social science. It is not brought on by relativists but by the pluralistic experience itself. This type of relativism has an impact whether social science propounds this theory.

But social science, in its study of comparative culture, gathers extensive data and clarifies issues relating to these phenomena. It provides the concepts through which relativity becomes part of the intellectual tradition of the society. It provides an awareness of the implications of cultural relativity for those who are exposed to the traditions in education, even though they might not otherwise experience or understand the impact of pluralism.

Therefore, it is reasonable to conclude that cultural relativism is not just an idea someone has had, but an interpretative response to experiences. To say that these experiences will in the future become more pervasive is only to note that the impact of cultural relativity can be expected to increase rather than decrease. What benefits, then, will be gained by Christians who accept relativity, are informed about it, and attempt to utilize it?

First, rather than destroying objective truth, cultural relativity is helpful in identifying it. Absolutists have contended that it is destructive because by comparing cultural practices that are different and seeking to understand them, there is the implication that there is no way to find out what is really true or right. More importantly, when relativists insist that objective truth is found to be inter-subjective—the agreement of several subjective expressions—it undermines confidence that a human can ever hope to know with confidence what is really true.

The absolutists are right to the extent that the study of comparative cultures does show that some cultural beliefs and norms that we think to be necessary may not be. But what they have ignored is that this may help rather than hinder in the search for truth. In comparing cultures, we may discover that some cherished ideas must be relinquished, but we may also discover evidence that other aspects are crucial.

For example, references are often made to differences in the institution of the family across cultures. To some this knowledge is threatening. In other cultures there are different beliefs and norms about how many husbands or wives should be in a family, what responsibilities members have, and such matters as sexual norms. There may be an uneasy feeling that "temptations" lurk in this knowledge. Knowing that other people have other ways may make us less sure of our own. But this can be avoided only by isolation and ignorance. More importantly, to avoid knowledge of other ways prohibits the positive values to be gained from the knowledge of comparative cultures. It was by comparing family studies in varying cultures that it became possible to identify those necessary underlying functions that the family could best provide. George Hillery demonstrated an example of this by considering the findings in the studies of Israeli kibbutz life. His conclusion was that when all traditional functions are stripped away from family life, it still provides for social and sexual intimacy in a better way than could be provided by any other arrangement.[1] To see cultural relativity as only destructive is to see only part of its contribution. It does undermine some ideas considered to be objective, but it also leads to other insights and better understanding.

A second contribution is also one that absolutists consider to be detrimental. This is the demystifying function of cultural relativity. The application of cultural relativity to the study of any subject inevitably questions the claims of that subject that it has some unique insight about the world. To the believer of the insight who sees it as self-evidently and unambiguously true, such questioning is perceived to be subversive.

But Christianity is not the only view of reality challenged by cultural relativity. Atheism, agnosticism, communism, and other such systems of thinking, including secular humanism, are fervently believed by some individuals; but these are also demystified when examined from the perspective of cultural relativity. Their claims to a superior status cannot be sustained in the same light after such an examination.

Glover and Strawbridge have pointed out the tendency of classical sociologists such as Durkheim and Manheim to believe that their own sociological thinking was free of social influences.[2] Thomas Kuhn's *The Structure of Scientific Revolutions*, first published in 1962, continues to be very influential because of its thesis and the evidence it presents that the social characteristics in scientific groups— natural science included—is a very important force in what comes to be considered as scientific knowledge. The understanding of the relative nature of human knowledge applies to all sectors. It can be very helpful for Christians to perceive this characteristic of all forms of knowledge including that which is scientific or humanistic.

Probably the most important contribution occurs when cultural relativity demystifies contemporary views and their chronocentrism. In the chronocentric view, the current age is so superior that no one who lived two thousand years ago could provide any insights by which we may benefit today. But when this view is examined in the light of cultural relativity, it is reduced from its self-evident superiority to only one of many ways of defining reality. Its claim of superiority rests too much upon the fact that it is current. To illustrate, our current ways of utilizing inanimate energy for massive power sources producing industrial might are impressive. So also is the scientific cause and effect links that have led to so many inventions. But the knowledge we use as individuals to relate to each other, organize families, and develop communities does not demonstrate such superior insight. Indeed, is there any evidence of superiority at all in these practices? A systematic comparison of cultures poses the question of whether we have advanced at all in human relationships.

That cultural relativity can make us aware of our chronocentric prejudices and more receptive to the possibility that we can learn important insights from ancient people is an important advancement. It opens at least the possibility that a man two thousand years ago who never took a college course in science still might have had important insights into the process of human living. It can be an enormous contribution to the Christian effort if people will become less chronocentric; the grip of the contemporary is powerful and difficult to release.

The Christian absolutist will welcome the demystifying of other belief systems, but may still fear that if Christianity is subjected to this same process, the consequences would be destructive. But what is lost? Inevitably some views that we hold will be challenged and discarded. Certainly, any claims that the history of the churches has been one of uncorrupted service to humanity will have to be abandoned. The collusion of the churches in the cultures of racism, nationalism, and empire building will have to be recognized and admitted. But these changes are not damaging. Indeed, they are better recognized and admitted. The Christian faith itself is not damaged because it rests upon events and not upon absolutes.

Does not Jesus demystify very well by anyone's standards? Subject his life to any cross-cultural perspective, examine its origins and its outcomes, put it into any framework of thought. What remains is a life and teaching that are remarkably compelling, and producing a culture that is undeniably a part of our heritage.

The third contribution stems from the use of cultural relativity to identify the origin, development, and function of cultural traits. It is unavoidable that Christians are both participants in a culture of Christianity and at the same time participants in the culture of their communities, states, and nations. Church members have internalized these cultural traits and "brought them to church." Similarly, the church when it acts will express elements of the culture of its society. Indeed, if it is to be relevant in its society, it must express itself in ways that are at least understandable to its society. This poses a major problem for all churches. They must seek to be faithful to the culture of Christianity that is separate from the culture of the society in which they exist. The two cultures are always intermixed.

Denominations bear the stamp of the culture of their origins. The pagentry and hierarchy of the Roman Catholic church, the pacifism of the Amish, and the annual church meeting of the Baptists all are examples that can be directly traced to the place and time when the denomination first developed. It is not happenstance that the pacifist churches in America originated at about the same time period in Europe. Similarly, the Restorationist churches—identified as Christian Churches and Churches of Christ—grew out of an early nineteenth-century American frontier. Cultural traits from the society have become imbedded in the traditions of these Christian movements.

The appreciation of culture and sensitivity to the development of cultural traits that emerge with cultural relativity can contribute to the ability to distinguish concepts derived from Christian origins and those which have evolved from the society. Robert Bellah's essay on "civil religion" sought to identify the phenomenon in which the symbols of Christianity had been combined with the symbols of America.[3] This concept has been valuable in focusing attention on both the way in which traits of religion can become a part of the civil society and also how traits of society can be incorporated into the religious culture.

Because cultural relativity seeks to understand beliefs and norms within culture, it provides a method for identifying and distinguishing these traits and the role of each in the culture. The awareness of cultural processes that results from this emphasis can be a valuable contribution in understanding a Christian tradition and distinguishing those elements that originate within society. Expressed in Christian terms, this contribution aids in separating the Christian traits from worldliness.

A fourth contribution is that cultural relativity provides a critique of Christianity. This is, of course, precisely what many believers do not like about it. But this does not mean that it is not a contribution. It only means that this is a "medicine" that tastes awful and is avoided if possible. Christianity is not unusual in disliking this. But the power of Christian leaders and organizations is also a problem. If we accept the axiom that power corrupts, there is every reason to believe that Christian leaders are just as likely to be tempted with the corrupting influence of power as are other figures of power. The history of the church supports this thesis. Relevant critiques that identify the elements of culture and their functions can provide an effective way of counteracting some of these temptations. The demystification of the claims of Christian traditions does not destroy the message of Christ or the claims of the acts of God, but it does neutralize the pomposity and corruption that is often found among those who have religious power.

When social science is seen only as an enemy to be defeated or at least walled out, nothing is learned. However, when social science is perceived to be a study of human behavior from which insight may be gained, there is a potential for growth. With this approach, what at first may have seemed to be a destructive critique may be discovered to be helpful in gaining new insights. Freud's critiques of religion and his concepts of neurosis have been attacked as anti-Christian. But careful consideration of what he wrote has also led to the realization that Freud's work could be useful in helping Christians to understand more fully the biblical teaching on sin. In attempting to explore the unconscious, its effect upon behavior, and the strategies by which the ego develops defense mechanisms, Freud was unwittingly helping Christian scholars to take more seriously and explore more realistically the depths of sin. In Freud's work about the "psychopathology of everyday life," Christians can benefit from the insights on sin in everyday life. This is not to say that Christians should embrace all that a social scientist states. But it is to say that such critiques can be very beneficial, even if they are disturbing.

Cultural relativity, I contend, leads to a better perception of the nature of knowledge. As such it can reveal new importance to the biblical statement from Paul that our knowledge is partial.[4] According to the Biblical account, the Serpent in the Garden of Eden tempted Eve with the desire to have the knowledge of God.[5] That would seem to mean—in contemporary terms—that to desire the absolute truth rather than the partial, limited, and relative knowledge of humans is a temptation to evil. Indeed, this demand for full knowledge can be considered to be a refusal of faith. Any critique of the Christian faith from the point of view of cultural relativity need not be accepted with acquiescence any more than the view of Freud. It does provide, however, the opportunity for the Christian to listen and learn. The critique can be invaluable in reminding the Christian of the limitations of human knowledge.

The fifth contribution stems from the development of cross-cultural communication skills. Cultural relativity insists that if we are to understand someone we must have respect for, listen to, and learn very carefully about that person's culture. A good anthropological education includes experience in an alien culture. Anthropologists consider that only from such an experience can the skill develop to understand one's native culture. The accounts of mistakes in cross-cultural communication are legion. Every person who attempts such communication makes them. But the person who crosses the boundaries of cultures with ethnocentric confidence is likely to make more and too often even be unaware that they have been made.

If Christians are going to attempt to "make disciples" in every culture, there will be benefits in exercising sensitivity to cultural differences. To be defensive to social science is to cut oneself off from a large number of people who are intimately involved in precisely the types of skills that the Christian needs to carry out effectively the "great commission" given by Jesus. To communicate will require what Kosuke Koyama terms, "waterbuffalo theology." He writes of his efforts to communicate the Christian message to Thai farmers. It was only by sensing the life experiences of following a water buffalo through the paddies that he felt he could begin to understand how to communicate the Christian message.[6] It is this sensitivity to the culture of others, linked with an understanding of cultural processes and relativity, that can provide tremendous resources in the ever-difficult task of communicating across cultural lines.

In conclusion, none of these contributions occur inevitably. Learning about cultural relativity does not guarantee benefits. So also, many people who reject cultural relativism will practice these benefits—sometimes in an exemplary fashion. There are Christian missionaries, for example, who know nothing of cultural relativism yet practice it in their personal and ministerial lives. Unfortunately, however, there are many who do not. What I suggest is that cultural relativity and sensitivity to the points that it makes will increase awareness and is potentially very valuable. Careful, systematic consideration of relativity can improve the effectiveness of the Christian experience. Not only can a Christian negotiate better by making use of cultural relativism, there is also good reason to believe that there are benefits in doing so.

13

Can a Social Scientist Believe in Christianity?

It is not apparent that one who knows that his concepts are not
universal must also doubt that they are concepts of the universal.
Or, that one who understands how all of his experience is
historically mediated must believe that nothing is mediated through
history.

—H. Richard Niebuhr

We now look in the opposite direction and focus upon sociologists and the possibility that they can participate in the Christian faith. The answer to the title question must be affirmative, as there are a number of sociologists who are Christian believers. There is also an organization for such persons known as the Christian Sociological Society. It meets during the annual meetings of the American Sociological Association, publishes a newsletter, and carries on other activities. In recent years, at least two books of readings have been published that provide a total of sixty articles on different aspects of sociology from a Christian perspective.[1] These are not individuals who advocate Christianity from some vague humanistic concern that "everyone ought to have some religion." Rather, they represent Christian believers who are clearly within the traditional beliefs of the faith.

In spite of this, there is a sense in which the answer would seem to be negative. This seems evident in the writings of the Christian sociologists themselves. They seem like other Christians often do in simply asserting the truth of their knowledge without establishing any basis for the assertion. For example, William L. Smith-Hinds writes in the book edited by DeSanto that there are four kinds of knowledge: scientific, rational, intuitive, and revealed.[2] The "revealed" refers to the Bible, but upon what basis this can be a reliable source of knowledge compared to other writings is never discussed. Similarly, in an introduction the authors assert without any supporting evidence that the Christian view is the standard against which sociology is to be judged. For example, "The Christian's main concern with any model is whether or not the model squares realistically with Christian conceptions of human nature and needs."[3] To cite another example, Milton Reimer wrote about the Christian perspective on sociology, "[It] requires the subordination of [sociology] to the authority of the Scriptures."[4]

To traditional sociology, this begs the question. It asserts as fact what needs to be first established. In their writings, these Christians are explicit in the critiques of empiricism as only one among a number of ways of knowing. They either say nothing or are extremely vague in specifying other ways of knowing and how one can substantiate the knowledge gained through other methods. When we rely only on the assertion that the Bible's teachings are another way of knowing and demand that all other knowledge must be subordinate to it, we are practicing a dogmatic approach. When that approach is taken, the wall of separation between sociologists and Christians seems realistic. With this approach, in spite of the presence of Christian sociologists, the answer would seem to be that sociologists, as such, cannot be Christian believers.

But this may only be true because the case has been poorly stated. The wall is necessary because neither side can communicate convincingly with the other. But the question needs to be asked in a different way: is there a way for sociologists to consider and accept the traditional Christian beliefs without subordinating their sociology and being required to accept dogmatic assertions? An adequate answer to this is beyond the scope of this book, yet it is a reasonable question to ask.

With the objective of suggesting a tentative answer, the following excursion into the sociologist's world will now be undertaken. There are certain characteristics of the social scientist that are admirable but that may also become occupational hazards. That is, they carry within their practice traits that may interfere with other facets of the social scientist's life. Sociology, for example, was earlier referred to as "a debunking science." The sociologist is someone who sees through pretenses to reality. How can social processes be well understood if the sociologist simply takes at face value whatever is presented? This is also an important trait for others. We live in a world of misrepresentation, though we may be oblivious to it. We read in the newspaper as "news" a release from a public relations office. A hamburger chain advertises that it has the "best eatin' around." They and everyone else knows this is untrue. But we give it no thought and are, in fact, influenced by the advertising though it is demonstrably false. Corporations would not spend millions of dollars for advertising if they did not have proof of its effectiveness. If this characteristic was limited to these relatively unimportant matters it would not be worth noting. But it is not.

It can be an occupational hazard when it becomes, instead of a strategy for doing good sociology, a chronic personality characteristic. When this happens, the sociologist becomes unable to devote effort toward establishing the social ties, organizations, and institutions that humans need. Expert at "seeing through" all human efforts, the sociologist becomes unable to participate in these common social endeavors. Whenever such activities are attempted, the sociologist finds that there are always aspects of these endeavors that can be discounted. Such an individual can become unable to participate with commitment in Christian activities. This is not simply because the activities are Christian. The sociologist would be equally unable to participate in other types of endeavors. The reason is because there are always aspects of the organization that are "seen through," thus are questionable, and the sociologist withdraws. While this portrayal may be extreme, it does identify a very real occupational hazard and one that in varying degrees seems to be widespread. Sociologists tend not to be active with any degree of commitment in community organizations.

A preoccupation with knowledge can also be an occupational hazard. The question of the reliability of what is "known" is basic. The scientific method is accepted by the sociologist because it provides a way to justify conclusions and to allow others to examine the process by which the conclusions were reached. No individual can simply accept everything that is proposed as knowledge without some type of critical evaluation. We all must choose among competing claims.

For the sociologist, however, the critique of what passes as knowledge is inherent in all research and teaching. The more carefully and completely the justification for what can be known is developed, the better the work. Sociologists, like anyone, may at times be naive and gullible. But they are not supposed to be. The standards of science are supposed to prevail, and the sociologist is expected to be careful and critical in examining all of the information to determine what is true.

To such a person, the dogmatic assertions that the Bible is the way of knowing and sociological knowledge must be subordinated to it is unacceptable. How can a person substantiate this claim? As long as Christians rely upon these assertions, the occupational emphasis upon substantiated knowledge will hinder sociologists from being willing to consider seriously the Christian faith. Until and unless Christians can develop a way of knowing that can be justified, social scientists will be resistent.

A first step toward resolving this issue is to address the meaning of empirical knowledge. In the broader sense of the word, most knowledge is to some extent empirical. That is, in most instances, what is said to be known makes sense related to what a person experiences in his social world. If it is accepted on the authority of another, the acceptance occurs because the experience of the person has been that this other person has legitimate authority to speak on the subject. People may differ completely from us in what they think is true, but they hold to their truths because they make sense within the context of their own life experiences. This use of empirical knowledge may not be sufficient for scientific data but it is, in fact, just the kind of data the sociologist uses to make sense of the world when not doing research.

Christians also utilize empirical knowledge in this same way. When told not to speak further concerning Jesus, the apostles Peter and John responded, "We cannot but speak the things which have been seen and heard."[5] Their appeal was to empirical knowledge. The Bible portrays that the witness of the existence of God is found in the empirical experience of productive food supplies.[6] The biblical appeal to faith was also an appeal to empirical events and experiences.

The question then turns to whether there is an empirical path to Christian faith for the sociologist. One possible path is in the concept already discussed of perceiving Christianity as a culture: by using the tools of the sociologist's craft, how can the existence of Christianity be understood? From that small, ancient band of Israelites several thousand years ago who thought God had chosen them, to the current time when we see Christian faith advancing and retreating in various parts of the earth—what can sociological analysis tell us? It is an empirically verifiable fact that both Jewish and Christian faiths exist. There are corroborative lines of evidence that Christianity began about two thousand years ago in the land of the Jews. What can be learned?

The sociologist will quickly recognize that this is not the method by which most sociology of religion is studied. Religion is seen as a category of phenomena, and Christianity is one case of many in the general phenomena. It is assumed that religion is a category of cases that have common characteristics. Thus fundamentalism—whether Muslim, Buddhist, or Christian—will share common social characteristics. The encounter of orthodoxy with modernity will involve similar processes whatever the religion may be. There is nothing wrong with these approaches. They represent good sociology, and they lead to important insights. But the prevalence of this type of study can lead to the neglect of alternative types. In particular, it neglects the approach advocated by Max Weber who recognized that every social phenomenon had a unique history, set of social circumstances, and social processes.[7]

If Judaism and Christianity are approached as social phenomena, we are involved in what can be a fascinating quest. For the unbelieving sociologist, the Bible is a central source because it is the written record of the people of this faith and not because it is necessarily a perfect revelation. The primitive society of the Old Testament is recorded as one in which semi-nomads lived. So also is the record of nation-building. Ancient people came into contact with other cultures. Their policies were sometimes wise, sometimes unwise, often a matter of muddling through. And sometimes they did not get through at all. They said God had chosen them and that they would survive to bless all of the people of the world. And then there is Christianity. It appeared as a sect of the Jews. It was obviously based upon the Jewish culture, yet it was also very different.

These lines do not suggest the conclusions of such a study, but they are intended to suggest the type of bridge from empirical knowledge to the Christian faith that is available. With this empirical approach, the sociologist does not find in the Bible the expected dogmatic assertions and absolutist declarations. Rather, he finds a record of events and people dealing with those events.

It is not that dogmatic assertions are necessarily wrong. Rather, it is that when they are unsupported assertions, they are unpersuasive to the outsider. Does anyone really believe in the miracles of the Bible or the Bible as being a perfect revelation because someone claims it is so? Miracles have been claimed as support for many assertions. Forget the dogmatic assertions and the declarations of absolutism. Let Abraham, Moses, Jesus, and Paul tell their own events. It is not empirically verifiable that Jesus arose from the dead. It is empirically verifiable, however, that shortly after that time in which the Bible says Jesus arose from the dead there were people who were ready to die for this truth of their faith. The question of the nature of that faith is a reasonable one to pursue. Ultimately, as I have suggested, the question for Christianity resolves itself in an answer to the question: "What do you think of the Christ?"[8]

No sociologist can have all of the data desired to answer this question. But that is true of all questions. There are some empirical bridges to the question that allow for the development of an opinion. It is my own experience that when posed in this manner, there is a compelling reason for traditional Christian commitment. I find the record of the Bible and the life of Jesus to be more compelling than I sense some absolutists do in their declarations that dogmatic, absolutist assertions are supremely important. When the events of the biblical record are found to be compelling and an individual has positive experiences with Christians, the traditional doctrines also make sense. They are believed, but not because they can be scientifically proved or because they are dogmatically asserted. They are believed because they are the natural consequences of conclusions that have already been reached.

The questions discussed here have been asked by many, but they have not been asked by sociologists. Undoubtedly, many are not interested in asking—or, at least, not interested enough to pursue them to their conclusion. But some may be willing, and when they are, there is common ground to explore. If this common ground is workable, then the sociologist can negotiate the questions of the Christian faith and retain the integrity of the sociological commitment. The usual factors that keep people away from Christian commitment will still be operative. But the possibility of making that commitment will have been markedly improved. Subordination to dogmatic assertion of absolutes is unnecessary. Thus, the wall is unnecessary.

14

The Contributions of Christianity to Social Science

> The people in Wilde's plays were dominated by fashion; everyone
> was in a fever to do what was being done nowadays.
> —Emilie Griffin

If the social scientist can negotiate without the wall, what benefits might there be? Our focus now is upon those possible contributions that the social scientist may gain by being a Christian. More specifically, it is to see how the culture that exists among social scientists can benefit by contact with the cultural tradition which the Christian faith conveys.

If Christianity is beneficial to an individual, then—by definition—the sociologist as an individual would benefit by being a Christian. But this chapter is not a consideration of the personal value of Christian faith. Rather, it is to identify some examples of benefits that Christianity as a culture can make to the particular needs of social science as a culture.

Similarly, I am not giving a priori superior status to Christianity. Though Christians often insist upon this, the insistence is destructive to communication. It reinforces the wall rather than encouraging understanding. It raises fears among social scientists that Christians still possess the mentality of the age when the church defined what was permissible for scientists to think. For Christians to be committed to its truth and to consider these truths to be superior in importance is appropriate. But to demand that scientists accept a subordinate position for the epistemology of their science inevitably develops fear and defensiveness on the part of the scientists.

An example of this demand for priority can be found in Grunlan's comments concerning a Christian perspective on sociology:

> Any approach to sociology that ignores the biblical account of the origin of humans and its implications, as well as the effects of the fall and the potential of redemption, will always come short of the full truth. An

understanding of the scriptural view of human nature is essential for a valid sociology.[1]

The epistemological arrogance of the statement is shocking. Instead of the biblical statement of the Apostle Paul that "I know in part,"[2] Grunlan suggests that full truth is available, if sociologists will accept his conditions. He prescribes that a valid sociology must incorporate doctrines from the Bible. To be valid, then, sociology—as sociology—must submit itself to the views of reality from Christian faith. Carl F. H. Henry similarly insists that the evangelical Christian "emphasizes the absolute character of revelation while it views the assertions of science skeptically."[3] Such interpretations almost insure that sociologists will ignore any contributions Christians might otherwise make. The potential value of the ideas Grunlan and Henry specify will be ignored when presented in this manner.

The contribution of Christianity to sociology can occur when Christians enter into dialogue, present their own ways of knowing and their conclusions, and respect the work of the social sciences. In such a setting, Christians can offer meaningful and constructive critiques of the social scientific enterprise and can make very real contributions. In so doing, one important contribution can be that of providing sociology a reminder that it is itself subject to the same effects of social processes as are the subjects of its study.

It would seem that Christians should support the criteria of science that all ideas should be made as explicit as possible and be subject to critical evaluation. This is valuable in sorting through the multitude of ideas represented to be facts. It is a biblical commandment that Christians are not to "believe every spirit but test the spirits to see whether they are of God."[4] This is reason enough for Christians to be in the forefront of those who seek not only to critique but to welcome being critiqued. It is counterproductive when Christians consider that it is fair to critique sociology and yet are unwilling to be critiqued by sociologists.

Christians cannot consider beliefs to be off-limits to criticism. Though Christians disagree with much of the criticism, it can still be received with thoughtfulness and graciousness. Only if Christians can welcome the criticisms of sociology can there be hope that sociologists will pay attention to the criticisms from Christians. It is in such give-and-take that Christians can make very real contributions to the social sciences.

An area in which sociologists need reminding that they also are subject to social processes is inherent in the dangers of chronocentrism. The history of sociology is usually traced to Auguste Comte. This means that at the earliest, "sociological insights" are considered to have begun in the later half of the nineteenth century. Durkheim's study of suicide, though recognized to have been flawed, is considered to be the finest early example of real empirical research. It wa published in 1897. Whether one agrees with these particular designations, the point remains the same: the serious study of the history of sociology consists of a history of not more than one hundred years. Even this overstates the time span, because it is usually considered that the important empirical social research is the most recent.

There are, of course, sociologists who acknowledge that there have been some outstanding thinkers throughout the ages who wrote down their insights. Although these insights were not derived from systematic data of the type that sociologists today prefer, they were based upon observations that others made of the world in which they lived. They may have been, in fact, more accurate and insightful than many of the conclusions derived from pouring over a list of regression coefficients produced by a computer. But while some are very aware of this, sociology, as it is usually presented, has not really paid attention to social theorists from past times. Real sociology is considered to be current sociology. Such thinking is inherently chronocentric.

Christianity has a vested interest in making the case that ideas from other times should not be automatically discounted or ignored because they have been around for centuries. Ideas—including ancient ideas—should be considered on the basis of their own merit rather than ignored because of their age. Christian scholars should be sensitive to the possibility of chronocentric attitudes and from this sensitivity be capable of reminding the sociologists that they are no less susceptible to the temptations of chronocentrism than are others. Indeed, the perceived need of sociologists to prove that they are fully scientific in the eyes of their fellow disciplines, as well as funding agencies, may promote a temptation to chronocentrism beyond that which would otherwise exist.

The cultural relativity that shakes the foundations of knowledge needs to be applied to this chronocentrism of sociology as well as to other areas of knowledge. For example, one potential area for exploration is the concept of sin: it is extremely rare for sociologists and anthropologists to use a concept that is even roughly equivalent to the Christian notion of sin.[5] Christians may demand that sociologists think in terms of sin and criticize the sociologists for their refusal to do so. But there are alternative approaches. Christians might investigate why sociologists do not use the concept. Is it because sociologists have some empirical evidence that renders the concept meaningless or mistaken? Is it because sociologists have found that humans do not purposely inflict harm and suffering on other humans? Is such harm as is inflicted found to be only a result of ignorance, illness, or cultural conflict?

Sociology can point to many situations where the concept of sin has been used in ways that were destructive. But apart from these, there is ample evidence that there is a persistent inflicting of suffering in family, organizational, community, and national conflict. The discipline of sociology has not addressed the questions that such events seem to invite. Indeed, when considered in the context of cultural relativity using comparative cultures, sociology seems amazingly unwilling to deal directly with the inhumanity of humans.

Why do sociology texts continue to write of socialization and deviance as processes without any sense of the anguish that is so pervasive and widespread in the contemporary world? Is it not likely that this characteristic of sociology grows out of the optimism of that age when sociology was being developed? Science was pushing back the curtain of ignorance, and social science was going to do away with conflict by the application of its empirical knowledge. In this, sociology also is a product of its culture.[6] Its choice of subject matter and traditions for formulating and considering its subject matter is, to a large extent, conditioned by its own cultural evolution. Just as the Roman Catholic church developed a structure reflecting the hierarchy of the Roman empire and Mennonites developed a peace witness growing out of their early social experiences, so sociology also reflects the culture of the age in which its traditions were established.

Sociology is not a field of knowledge divorced from being relative to culture. It has a powerful epistemology but its real-life situation is not separate from the usual cultural processes because of this. It is misleading, then, to think that because sociology is science, it should not be considered in the light of its own cultural evolution. The recognition that sociology is relative does not mean that faith in sociology is destroyed. It does create a consciousness that sociology, like other knowledge systems, should be subject to careful scrutiny. Sociologists tend not to provide this scrutiny, though there are some sociologists who are active in the sub-area called the "sociology of sociology." Their work, however, does not reflect issues that Christian sociologists might explore.

The idea that any group of people will be adequately self-critical is a proposition that should be scrutinized carefully. There is much critical debate among sociologists, but sociologists are not critically examining many crucial areas. Examples of the few analyses that have been made of textbooks have demonstrated some of the problems emanating from a lack of sufficient evaluation.[7]

That such a lack could have occurred is probably less important than the more fundamental issues to which sociologists fail to give attention. The sociologist's own socialization into the discipline simply glosses over them. The culture of sociology will define a world for the sociologist in such a way that it will obscure some issues as well as clarify other issues. It may be that an outsider or a marginal member can notice these and bring them to the attention of the discipline. Sociologists recognize this in the study of other cultures. It is no less true of their own.

If there is truth in the saying that "power corrupts and absolute power corrupts absolutely," it applies to the sociologist no less than to a political dictator or Christian leader. But do sociologists have power? Sociologists do not think of themselves as powerful. There are too many funding agencies and corporate employers who do not recognize and reward the contributions that the sociologist can make. Sociologists, rather, are more attuned to feeling a sense of powerlessness than of power. But when it comes to self-image regarding the conventional world, the situation is quite different. Here the sociologist "sees through" the conventional interpretations of reality. Thus in regard to the Christian, the sociologist has a sense of epistemological power. The sociologist thinks he knows how he knows. The sociologist does not think that the Christian does. Such confidence blinds. And if there is blinding, the sociologist is operating with a closed capacity. Again, the Christian's critique, appropriately presented, can be of immense benefit.

A second major type of contribution is in the prevention of social science's tendencies to dehumanize. This requires of Christians a certain humanistic interest. Humanism, as it is used here, means a concern for human well-being and does not mean a denial of God. It means a humanism in which Christians love the world following the example of God who loved the world.[8] Christians, therefore, should develop an effective opposition to those elements that dehumanize.

In this contribution, Christians are not involved in opposing social science. It is not a matter of speaking a different language across a wall. It is a matter of being involved in the work of the sociologist, not a matter of attempting to dictate conditions to the sociologist from a superior position. Christians have also played a part in dehumanizing processes. Therefore, Christians do not occupy a superior position. But Christians can walk with sociologists and, out of a love for the world, point out implications in the sociologists' work that may not be evident to those within the culture of sociology.

One author's identification of dehumanizing potential in the contemporary emphases has been stated in the following way:

> In the complex web that makes up a society, where elements of the past mingle with activities of the present and hopes, fears or aspirations for the future, there are vital elements that are resistant, if not impervious to quantification. These include, for example, myth, ritual, and symbol. . . . To overlook or exclude these elements is to impoverish the inquiry, and at an even more fundamental level to misrepresent what we are about. By its postulates and its techniques of inquiry, behavioral science has become not merely trivial, but in an elemental sense anti-social.[9]

Christians have made similar observations. But too often it was from the vantage point of attack. Why not become involved in the search? In this sense the Christian is asking questions, looking for implications, and noting where a line of thought logically leads. Quantification has provided precision in the analysis of data. What important factors must be omitted when quantification is the standard? How does this impoverish the understanding? In what ways does this end up, in its effect, as anti-social?

Asking the sociologist to examine what social values are beneficial to the development of meaningful groups will provide normative systems and enrich the life experiences of its members. This is the plea McGehee has made to sociology, calling for sociology to define humans as a subject of life rather than an object. It is, in other words, to call for sociology to contribute its expertise to the development and strengthening of social structures which can be productive for the human experience.[10] To see through the facades of social organization is valuable, but it is not an appropriate final objective. Humans need myth, ritual, and symbol that is meaningful and socially integrative. To be only a "debunking science" is to fail to provide the type of scientific contribution that can be part of the building of a social world. It can be a Christian contribution to walk with the social scientists, point out real human needs, and urge them toward working on the more important questions.

Another example of contribution could be in the exploration of the effect of materialism on society. Christians have, of course, spoken frequently about the failure of materialism. But here again it has been more often in the form of attack. It is a different matter to be open to the findings of sociology and raise pertinent questions for further study. As I discussed in the third chapter, Peter Berger wrote in 1974, after experience in third world countries, that there was increasing evidence of the failure of materialism in both western societies and Marxist countries. Christians should be interested in this not just because it confirms what they already believe. Rather, it provides input that seems to corroborate what has been a part of their belief. It raises important questions. What is the evidence of this failure? How can it be confirmed or disproved? What happens as a consequence of the failure? Why have sociologists not been more aware of this failure if it is confirmed? In what ways can Christian alternatives be effectively made available in meeting the needs that such a failure creates?

Once again, I am trying to propose a scenario of the kind of approach Christians can make that will provide positive contributions to the work of the social sciences. Such contributions must avoid the errors of the dogmatic absolutistic approach that seeks to subordinate sociology, with Christians fully admitting that they also only know in part.

These illustrations, however, suggest a common agenda for the future. In a world where culture was once a rigid structure of social organization and norms were tightly defined, many humans found society oppressive. Sociology as a debunking science provided important relief for this by allowing such people to understand the human development of those rigid structures and the possibilities of alternatives. In a world where the institutions of the society have already been demythologized and where norms that govern behavior are vague, it may not be freedom that is desired, but direction. What is the role of the sociologist when people no longer believe in the institutions of society? To continue to debunk the institutions is to be irrelevant.

There is a need for a new approach that will look carefully at social meaning, at commitment, and at the construction of myths. The relevant question has become: how does society develop meaningful, productive groups, and how do people participate in these groups? At the core of the Christian religion is the challenge to Christian believers to devote themselves to care for the world. When this is translated into Christian scholarship, it can be an ongoing contribution to the social sciences. The potential is there but only if the Christian is talking with and listening to the world of the social scientist. If this occurs, the social scientist who listens can benefit. It cannot be accomplished if a wall divides them.

15

An Epilogue

You might as well fall flat on your face as lean too far over backward.

—James Thurber

To briefly review my original thesis, a mental and social wall separates Christians and cultural relativists. The wall is there because it has been perceived to be necessary. I contend that it is not only unnecessary but harmful.

Christians have believed it to be necessary because they have perceived that cultural relativism undermines the idea of objective truth that in turn, undermines not only the morals of a society but also the basis of the Christian faith itself. If that were true, the wall would certainly be necessary. Relativists have perceived that Christians, in their absolutism, are dogmatic and narrow. Relativists fear that absolutists wish to exercise control over thought, forcing it into subjection to the Christian dogmas. It has, as they know, happened in the past. They fear that the freedom of the social scientist to be a scientist is thus endangered by the absolutists. In this view, the wall is seen as important.

But cultural relativism could not prevent God from making a revelation. It also could not prevent people from considering and finding faith in that revelation. If God exists and desires to speak, God will certainly speak. Christian absolutists insist as a basic dogma that, in fact, God has spoken and it is available in the Bible. I examined the Bible and discovered that the biblical statements are not at odds with the view of knowledge expounded by cultural relativists.

The Bible corresponds more to cultural relativism than absolutism in its presentation of knowing. The biblical message is consistent with relativism in the general view of the process of revelation, in the interpretation of its basis, and in its view of the people of other religions. To be more specific: the general view of revelation was found in the process through which Abraham's descendants were separated from other cultures and developed a separate culture to provide a basis for Jesus' message. This is consistent with our knowledge of relativistic cultural processes but unnecessary for absolutistic interpretations. In the interpretation of its basis, God established himself not in absolute principles but in the events of humans. God announced himself to be the "God of Abraham," not the God of absolutistic assertions. The biblical view of the people of other religions was that God was not partial but just; that people were to be judged by whether they sought the truth and how they treated the least members of their society. Thus God's judgment was considered to be based upon that which people could know and not by standards of a religion with which they had had no contact.

These conclusions do not suggest that Christianity is just "one of the religions" or that its truth is compromised. Rather, they clarify the nature of the Christian religion and its truth. The Bible, by this interpretation, is considered as portraying Jesus as the revelation of God. This revelation is light to people who would otherwise live in darkness. The doctrines of Christianity are perceived as conveying this light and are the means by which people experience salvation. It insists that people who know that this is light, but who prefer darkness, are to be condemned. So also any person in any culture who rejects light for darkness would be condemned.

These conclusions avoid the dilemmas that seem so often to plague students of world religion. John Hick, for example, interpreted the statement that there was "salvation in no other name" than Jesus as the nerve of the old absolutist dogma. Yet he seems to have assumed, as have so many others, that this interpretation accurately reflected the absolutism of biblical religion and therefore had to be rejected. But Hick also rejects Rahner's view that "devout persons of other faiths [are] anonymous Christians"[1]—that people of a non-Christian religion who are faithful to that religion are really Christians. Hick finds both alternatives unsatisfactory. What he did not consider was the possibility—which I have contended is the reality—that the Bible does not take either approach. Adherents to other religions are neither anonymous Christians nor automatically condemned. The biblical view of a just God who judges all relative to the reality of their situations goes far beyond either category.

The Bible, indeed, provides an interpretation of its teaching that is consistent with a pluralistic world. It has provided ways of interpreting the relativities of human culture within its message. Central to this is the realization that Christianity itself is a culture. The biblical message states that God not only revealed his word but also provided for the development of a culture through which that message could be understood, believed, and conveyed. Cultural relativity is an aid in understanding this process. It is also an aid in relativizing the chronocentric and ethnocentric views that are so powerful in undermining Christian belief. It is in no sense an enemy of the faith. Instead, it is a friend that not only can help in understanding the Christian faith but can provide insight into competing ideas of truth. Not only is the wall unnecessary, it is undesirable.

Theologian J. I. Packer observes that "pressure on conservative theology is still building up from exponents of religious relativism and pluralism."[2] He rejects the liberal compromise of the past and argues for resistance. My contention is that relativism and pluralism are realities that must not be ignored. But neither relativism nor pluralism endanger either conservative theology or biblical faith, unless there is an insistence upon these false alternatives of compromise or resistance. It is once again a situation where we need to "catch up" with the Bible that squarely confronts both a pluralistic world and relativistic knowledge.

Notes

Chapter 1. Setting the Stage

1. James Davison Hunter, *American Evangelicalism: Conservative Religion and the Quandary of Modernity* (New Brunswick, N.J.: Rutgers University Press, 1983), 107. Hunter also cites Peter L. Berger, "Ethics and the New Class," *Worldview* (April 1978): 6–11; B. Bruce-Briggs, *The New Class?* (New Brunswick, N.J.: Transaction, 1979); Alvin Gouldner, "The New Class (Project 1 and 2)," *Theory and Society* (Fall 1978); and Irving Horowitz, "On the Expansion of New Theories and the Withering Away of Old Classes," *Society* 16 (1979): 55–62 for use of this concept.

2. Ibid., 108.

3. Eugene A. Nida and William Reyburn, *Meaning across Cultures* (Maryknoll, N.Y.: Orbis Books, 1981), 1–2.

4. Ronald A. Knox, *On Englishing the Bible* (London: Burns and Oates, 1949), 11.

5. Eleanor Bowen, *Return to Laughter* (New York: Harper, 1954).

6. An application of this in the issue of sociology and theology is William H. Swatos, Jr., "Literature and Lebensform: The Personal God as a Social Being," *Perspective in Religious Studies* 7 (1980): 38–49.

7. Elvin Hatch, *Culture and Morality: The Relativity of Values in Anthropology* (New York: Columbia University Press, 1983), 8.

8. Francis A. Schaeffer, *A Christian Manifesto*, rev. ed. (Westchester, Ill.: Crossway, 1982), 18.

9. Ibid., 21.

10. Ibid., 18.

11. Ernst Gellner, *Relativism and the Social Sciences* (Cambridge: Cambridge University Press, 1985), 83.

12. Paul Johnson, *Modern Times* (New York: Harper and Row, 1983), 419.

13. Joe Carson Smith, "Contextualization or Christ?" *Christian Standard* 114 (1979): 427.

14. Elton Trueblood, *The Common Ventures of Life* (Waco, Texas: Word Books, 1975), 113.

15. Charles H. Kraft, *Christianity in Culture: A Study in Dynamic Biblical Theologizing in Cross-Cultural Perspective* (Maryknoll, N.Y.: Orbis Books, 1979), 17.

16. Peter L. Berger, *A Rumor of Angels* (Garden City, N.Y.: Doubleday, 1969), 39–40.

17. Ibid., 38.

18. David Lyon, *Sociology and the Human Image* (Downers Grove, Ill.: Intervarsity Press, 1983), 107.

19. Jacob Bronowski, *The Ascent of Man,* (Boston: Little, Brown, 1973), 374.

20. Johnson, *Modern Times,* 201, 296.

21. Arthur Schlesinger, Jr., "Pretension in the President's Pulpit," *Wall Street Journal*, 17 March 1983, 3.

22. Keith A. Roberts, *Religion in Sociological Perspective* (Homewood, Ill.: Dorsey Press, 1974), 366.

23. *Humanist Manifestos I and II* (Buffalo, N.Y.: Prometheus Books, 1973), 17.

24. Ibid., 8.

25. Alfred McClung Lee, *Sociology for Whom?* (New York: Oxford University Press, 1978), 93.

26. Robert E. Webber, *Secular Humanism: Threat and Challenge* (Grand Rapids, Mich.: Zondervan, 1982), 47.

27. Emile Durkheim, *Elementary Forms of the Religious Life* (New York: The Free Press, 1965), 474.

28. Dietrich Bonhoeffer, *Letters and Papers from Prison* (New York: Macmillan, 1967), 195–97.

29. Andrew Greeley, *Unsecular Man: The Persistence of Religion* (New York: Schocken Books, 1972), 7.

30. See Robert C. Liebman and Robert Wuthnow, *The New Christian Right: Mobilization and Legitimation* (New York: Aldine Publishing Co., 1983); and Stuart Rothenberg and Frank Newport, *The Evangelical Voter: Religion and Politics in America* (Washington, D.C.: The Institute for Government and Politics, 1984).

31. Jerry Falwell, *The Old Fashioned Gospel Hour* (Television program, 22 May 1983).

32. Max Weber, *The Methodology of the Social Sciences* (New York: Free Press, 1949), 13.

Chapter 2. The Challenge of Science

1. William Grosvenor Pollard, *Physicist and Christian: A Dialogue between the Communities* (New York: Seabury, 1961), viii.

2. Ibid., 12.

3. Paul F. Parsons, "Reading, Writing, and a Way of Life," *Christianity Today* 7 November 1986, 35.

4. Ronald L. Johnstone, *Religion and Science in Interaction: The Sociology of Religion* (Englewood Cliffs, N.J.: Prentice-Hall, 1975), 4.

5. Ibid., 4.

6. Benton Johnson, "Sociological Theory and Religious Truth," *Sociological Analysis* 19 (1977): 368–88. This article has an excellent discussion of this issue.

7. Elizabeth K. Nottingham, *Religion: A Sociological View* (New York: Random House, 1971), 4.

8. William Dyrness, *Christian Apologetics in a World Community* (Downers Grove, Ill.: Intervarsity Press, 1983), 145–50.

9. National Commission on Excellence in Education, *A Nation at Risk: The Imperative for Educational Reform* (United States Department of Education, April 1983), 10.

10. Ernst Becker, *Escape from Evil* (New York: Free Press, 1975), 9.

11. Norman Cousins, *The Healing Heart* (New York: Norton, 1983), 28.

12. Carl R. Babbie, *Sociology: An Introduction* (Belmont, Calif.: Wadsworth, 1983), 35.

13. Peter L. Berger, *The Sacred Canopy,* (New York: Doubleday, 1967), 124–25.

14. Earl Sagan, *Cosmos* (New York: Random House, 1980), 4.

15. Richard A. Baer, Jr., "TV: Carl Sagan's Narrow View of the Cosmos," *Wall Street Journal*, 24 October 1980, 35.

Notes 159

Chapter 3. The Gauntlet Taken Up

1. Robert Zwier, *Born-Again Politics: The New Christian Right in America* (Downers Grove, Ill.: Intervarsity Press, 1982).
2. J. I. Pierard, "Focus on the New Right," *Christian Century*, 10 October 1984, 930.
3. Edward Dobson, "Christian Atheism," *Fundamentalist Journal*, February 1986): 12.
4. Jerry Falwell, *Listen America!* (Garden City, N.Y.: Doubleday, 1980), 206.
5. Jerry Falwell, *The Fundamentalist Phenomenon* (Garden City, N.Y.: Doubleday, 1981), 24.
6. Ibid., 186.
7. Ibid., 192.
8. Tim LaHaye, *The Battle for the Mind* (Old Tappan, N.J.: Fleming H. Revel, 1980), 225.
9. Ibid., 229.
10. Schaeffer, *A Christian Manifesto*, 18.
11. Ibid., 41.
12. Ibid., 133.
13. Ibid., 131.
14. Ibid., 134.
15. Gordon Kleiman, "Parents' Groups Purging Schools of Humanist Books and Classes," *New York Times*, 17 May 1981, 1.
16. Mackay-Smith, "Schools Are Becoming the Battleground in the Fight against Secular Humanism," 31.
17. Falwell, *The Fundamentalist Phenomenon*, 189–92.
18. Charles Colson, "Dear Pat: Winning Isn't Everything," *Christianity Today*, 21 November 1986, 60.
19. Ron Sider, "A New Covenant of Respect, Integrity, and Biblical Faithfulness," *Evangelicals for Social Action Newsletter*, November 1986: 1.
20. Peter L. Berger, *The Sacred Canopy* (New York: Doubleday, 1967), 164.
21. Peter L. Berger, *Pyramids of Sacrifice* (Garden City, N.Y.: Anchor, Doubleday, 1974), 42–43.
22. Falwell, *The Fundamentalist Phenomenon*, 186.
23. Ibid., 24.
24. Ibid., 89–90.
25. Richard Quinney, *Providence: The Reconstruction of Social and Moral Order* (New York: Longman, 1980), 5.
26. Ibid., 12.
27. Ibid., 6.
28. Ibid., 7.
29. Ibid., 5.
30. Hunter, *American Evangelicalism*, 112.
31. Harvey Cox, *Turning East* (New York: Simon and Schuster, 1977), 20.
32. Ibid., 17.
33. Ibid., 9.
34. Kathleen Agena, "The Return of Enchantment," *The New York Times Magazine*, 27 November 1983, 68.
35. Ibid.
36. Falwell, *The Fundamentalist Phenomenon*, 179–85. For the specific quotation, see page 183.
37. Ibid., 18.
38. Hunter, *American Evangelicalism*, 49.

Chapter 4. The Case for Cultural Relativity

1. David E. Hunter and Phillip Whitten, *Encyclopedia of Anthropology* (New York: Harper and Row, 1976), 102.

2. William R. Catton, "The Development of Sociological Thought," *Handbook of Modern Sociology*, Ed. Robert E. L. Faris (New York: Rand McNalley, 1964), 929.

3. Melvin Herskovitz, *Cultural Relativism: Perspectives in Cultural Relativism* (New York: Random House, 1972), 26.

4. Catton, "The Development of Sociological Thought," 930.

5. Hunter, *American Evangelicalism*, 16–17.

6. See Ephesians 5 : 25 for reference.

7. Hunter, *American Evangelicalism*, 28.

8. Hatch, *Culture and Morality*, 4.

9. See Anthony C. Thistleton, *The Two Horizons* (Grand Rapids, Mich.: William B. Eerdmans, 1980), 74.

10. Gordon Kaufman, *Relativism, Knowledge, and Faith* (Chicago: University of Chicago Press, 1960), 18.

11. Ibid., 15.

12. Ibid., 4.

13. Herskovitz, *Cultural Relativism*, 26.

14. Ibid., 64.

15. Ibid., 33.

16. Ibid., 64.

17. Albert Einstein, *Relativity: The Special and the General Theory* (New York: Crown Publishers, 1961), 16.

18. J. Daniel Hess, *From the Other Point of View* (Scottsdale, Pa.: Herald Press, 1980), 35–36.

19. Herskovitz, *Cultural Relativism*, 52.

20. Kraft, *Christianity in Culture*, 6.

21. Ibid., 10.

22. Ibid., 9.

23. Hatch, *Culture and Morality*, 35.

24. Clifford Geertz, "Distinguished Lecture: Anti Anti-Relativism," *American Anthropologist* 86 (June 1984): 263.

25. F. Allen Hanson, *Meaning in Culture* (Boston: Routledge and Keegan Paul, 1975), 37.

26. Hatch, *Culture and Morality*.

27. Geertz, "Distinguished Lecture: Anti Anti-Relativism," 264.

28. David Glover and Sheelagh Strawbridge, *The Sociology of Knowledge*, (Ormstirk, Lancashire: Causeway Press, 1985), 71–72.

29. William C. Shepherd, "Cultural Relativism, Physical Anthropology and Religion," *Journal for the Scientific Study of Religion* 19 (June 1980): 159.

30. Geertz, "Distinguished Lecture: Anti Anti-Relativism," 263.

31. Ibid., 264.

32. Shepherd, "Cultural Relativism, Physical Anthropology and Religion," 159–69.

33. Hatch, *Culture and Morality*, 104.

34. Ibid., 104.

35. Ibid., 105.

36. Ibid., 105.

37. Hanson, *Meaning in Culture*, 38.

38. Kaufman, *Relativism, Knowledge, and Faith*, 3.

39. Hanson, *Meaning in Culture,* 37.

40. Ibid., 41.

Chapter 5. Relativity in Context

1. Eugene Nida's writings are an example of this type of contribution. So also is Kraft, *Christianity in Culture;* and Kosuke Koyama, *Waterbuffalo Theology* (Maryknoll, N.Y.: Orbis Books, 1974).

2. Peter L. Berger, *The Heretical Imperative* (Garden City, N.Y.: Anchor, Doubleday, 1980), 26.

3. George W. Forell, *The Proclamation of the Gospel in a Pluralistic World: Essays on Christianity and Culture* (New York: Philadelphia: Fortress Press, 1973), 2–3.

4. Kraft, *Christianity in Culture,* 6.

5. Berger, *The Sacred Canopy,* 17.

6. Berger, *Invitation to Sociology,* 38.

7. Peter Burke, *Sociology and History* (Winchester, Mass.: Allen and Unwin, 1980), 19.

Chapter 6. The Absolutist Case against Cultural Relativity

1. Stephen A. Grunlan, "Biblical Authority and Cultural Relativity," in *Christian Perspectives on Sociology,* Eds. Stephen A. Grunlan and Milton Reimer (Grand Rapids, Mich.: Zondervan Publishing House, 1982).

2. Ibid., 52.

3. Kaufman, *Relativism, Knowledge, and Faith,* 4.

4. Johnson, *Modern Times,* 419.

5. LaHaye, *The Battle for the Mind,* 9.

6. Ibid., 34.

7. Carl F. H. Henry, *God, Revelation, and Authority,* vol. 1 (Waco, Texas: Word Books, 1976), 394.

8. Genesis 2:18.

9. Grunlan, "Biblical Authority and Cultural Relativity," 51.

10. Glover and Strawbridge, *The Sociology of Knowledge,* 67.

11. Matthew 5:9.

12. Matthew 10:34.

13. Bertrand Russell, *Why I am not a Christian and Other Essays on Religion and Related Subjects* (New York: Random House, 1957), 6–7.

14. Kaufman, *Relativism, Knowledge, and Faith,* 122.

15. Grunlan, "Biblical Authority and Cultural Relativity," 51.

16. See Stephen W. Stall, "Sociology of Knowledge, Relativism and Theology," In *Religion and the Sociology of Knowledge,* Ed. Barbara Hargrove (New York: The Edwin Mellon Press, 1984), 66–67.

17. Hatch, *Culture and Morality,* 99.

18. Ibid., 86.

19. Grunlan, "Biblical Authority and Cultural Relativity," 51.

20. Ibid., 51.

21. Kraft, *Christianity in Culture,* 120–31.

22. Ibid., 120.

23. Ibid., 125.

24. Ibid., 129.

25. Charles L. McGehee, "Spiritual Values and Sociology: When We Have Debunked Everything, What Then?" *American Sociologist* 17 (February 1982): 43.

Chapter 7. Relativity and Biblical Religion

1. John 14:6.
2. Acts 4:12.
3. LaHaye, *The Battle for the Mind*, 51.
4. Grunlan, "Biblical Authority and Cultural Relativity," 52.
5. Lyon, *Sociology and the Human Image*, 103–4.
6. Ibid., 107.
7. Kraft, *Christianity in Culture*, 11.
8. Galatians 4:4; Ephesians 1:10. See also Romans 5:6.
9. John 12:42.
10. Galatians 3:7; Romans 4:12.
11. John 8.
12. Berger, *The Heretical Imperative*, 109.
13. Ibid., 110.
14. Ibid., 17.
15. Ibid., 18.
16. Ibid., 96.
17. Buford Rhea, *The Future of the Sociological Classics* (London: George Allen and Unwin, 1981), ix.

Chapter 8. Old Testament Documents

1. Genesis 3.
2. Genesis 6:2.
3. Genesis 6:11–12.
4. Genesis 11:1–9.
5. Genesis 12:1–3.
6. Genesis 31:19.
7. Genesis 31:32–35.
8. Genesis 34.
9. Genesis 34:30.
10. Genesis 35:2.
11. Genesis 47:20–22.
12. Exodus 3:13.
13. Exodus 3:14–15.
14. Exodus 20:3–6.
15. Exodus 22:20.
16. Exodus 23:13.
17. Exodus 23:32–33.
18. Deuteronomy 7:5.
19. Deuteronomy 20:17–18.
20. Deuteronomy 17:2–5.
21. Deuteronomy 13.
22. Leviticus 26:28–33.
23. Joshua 24:2.
24. Joshua 24:14.
25. Exodus 32.
26. Judges 3:7; 10:6.
27. 1 Kings 11:1–8.
28. 1 Kings 12:25–31.
29. 2 Kings 17:9–18.
30. See as an example, the summary given in Nehemiah 9.

31. Deuteronomy 4:28.
32. Exodus 32.
33. Deuteronomy 4:33–35.
34. Deuteronomy 10:17.
35. Judges 6:31.
36. Judges 10:14.
37. 1 Kings 18:17–40.
38. 1 Kings 18:36.
39. 2 Kings 1:3.
40. Jeremiah 16:20.
41. Jeremiah 2:11.
42. Jeremiah 10:1–10.
43. Malachi 1:5.
44. Habakkuk 1:5.
45. Micah 4:5.
46. Zechariah 8:22–23. See also 2:5; 12:5; and Micah 4:1–4.
47. Zephaniah 3:1.
48. Malachi 1:11.
49. Zechariah 14:9.

Chapter 9. New Testament Documents

1. Matthew 28:19.
2. Acts 1:8.
3. John 1:49.
4. Mark 5:7.
5. Mark 15:26.
6. John 18:36.
7. Matthew 10:5.
8. John 1:1–3.
9. John 1:9.
10. Luke 24:46–47.
11. Matthew 28:19–20.
12. John 4:9.
13. Mark 7:25–30.
14. Luke 10:30–37.
15. Matthew 8:10–12. See also Luke 7:9.
16. Matthew 21:43.
17. John 14:6.
18. John 3:18–19.
19. Matthew 10:32–33. See also Luke 12:8.
20. Luke 6:47–49.
21. John 18:37.
22. John 7:17.
23. Luke 12:41–49.
24. Luke 12:47–48.
25. John 4:21–24.
26. Matthew 25:31–46.
27. John 14:6.
28. Acts 10:2.
29. Acts 11:1–3.
30. Acts 11:20.
31. Acts 10:34–35.

32. Acts 13:46.
33. Acts 14:16–17.
34. Acts 17:22.
35. Acts 17:26–31.
36. Acts 4:12.
37. Romans 1:16–18.
38. Romans 1:19–21.
39. Romans 2:14–16. Compare with the comments at Lystra, Acts 14:16–17.
40. Matthew 22:34–40.
41. Matthew 25:31–46.
42. Romans 3:29–30.
43. James 4:17.
44. Romans 14:5.
45. Romans 14:23.
46. Romans 14:14.
47. 1 Corinthians 3:11.
48. Romans 3:30.
49. 1 Corinthians 10:19–20.
50. 2 Corinthians 6:14–16.
51. 2 Thessalonians 1:8.
52. 2 Thessalonians 1:5–6.
53. 2 Peter 3:7.
54. 2 Peter 3:3.

Chapter 10. An Interpretation of the Review

1. Alan Peshkin, *God's Choice: The Total World of a Fundamentalist School* (Chicago: University of Chicago Press, 1986), 6.
2. Kenneth S. Kantzer, "A Man of Zeal and Contradiction," *Christianity Today*, 20 September 1985: 36–38. See also, *Christianity Today*, "Evangelical Leaders Judge Tony Campolo's Theology," 13 December 1985: 52–54.
3. J. I. Packer, "Good Pagans and God's Kingdom," *Christianity Today*, 7 January 1986: 24.
4. Romans 3:1.
5. Romans 3:2.
6. Galatians 4:8–9.
7. 1 Thessalonians 1:9.
8. 1 Peter 2:9.
9. Luke 12:47–48.
10. Matthew 25:31–46.

Chapter 11. Can a "Believer" Accept Cultural Relativity?

1. Glover and Strawbridge, *The Sociology of Knowledge*, 56.
2. Matthew 5:17.
3. Luke 9:49–50.
4. Hebrews 12:1–2.
5. Matthew 22:42.

Chapter 12. The Contributions of Cultural Relativism for Christian Belief

1. George A. Hillary, Jr., *Communal Organizations: A Study of Local Societies* (Chicago: University of Chicago Press. 1968), 178–79.

2. Glover and Strawbridge, *The Sociology of Knowledge,* 61.
3. Robert N. Bellah, "Civil Religion in America," *Daedalus* 96 (1967): 1–21.
4. I Corinthians 13:12.
5. Genesis 3.
6. Koyama, *Waterbuffalo Theology.*

Chapter 13. Can a Social Scientist Believe in Christianity?

1. Charles P. DeSanto, et al., *A Reader in Sociology: Christian Perspectives* (Scottsdale, Pa.: Herald Press, 1980); and Stephan A. Grunlan and Milton Reimer *Christian Perspectives on Sociology* (Grand Rapids, Mich.: Zondervan Publishing House, 1982).
2. DeSanto, et al.; ibid., 43.
3. Ibid., 14.
4. Grunlan and Reimer, "The Study of Sociology: An Introduction," 20.
5. Acts 4:20.
6. Acts 14:17.
7. Weber, *The Methodology of the Social Sciences,* 169–75.
8. Matthew 22:42.

Chapter 14. The Contributions of Christianity to Social Science

1. Stephen A. Grunlan, "Sociology and the Christian," *Christian Perspectives on Sociology,* eds. Stephen A. Grunlan and Milton Reimer (Grand Rapids, Mich.: Zondervan Publishing House, 1982), 411–12.
2. 1 Corinthians 13:12.
3. Henry, *God, Revelation, and Authority,* vol. 1, 174.
4. 1 John 4:1.
5. For excellent works that are the rare exceptions, see Stanford Lyman, *The Seven Deadly Sins: Society and Evil* (New York: St. Martins Press, 1983); Becker, *The Structure of Evil* and *Escape from Evil;* and Edward A. Ross *Sin and Society: An Analysis of Latter-Day Iniquity* (Boston: Houghton, Mifflin and Co., 1907).
6. See Lyman and Vidich, *American Sociology* (New Haven: Yale University Press, 1985); and William H. Swatos, Jr., *Faith of the Fathers: Science, Religion, and Reform in the Development of Early American Sociology!* (Bristol, Ind.: Wyndham Hall Press, 1984).
7. For examples, see Dean S. Dorn, "The ASA Code of Ethics and Textbooks in Sociology," *Teaching Newsletter* 8 (October 1983): 6–7; Graham B. Spenier and Catherine S. Stump, "The Use of Research in Applied Marriage and Family Textbooks" *Contemporary Sociology* 7 (1978): 553–62; and R. C. Hedley and T. C. Traweggia, "Urges Revision of Ethical Code to Include Teaching and Student Rights" *Footnotes* 5 (October 1977): 2–4.
8. John 3:16.
9. Edmond S. Ions, *Against Behaviorism,* (Totowa, N.J.: Rowman and Littlefield, 1977), 154–155.
10. McGehee, "Spiritual Values and Sociology," 43.

Chapter 15. An Epilogue

1. John Hick, *God Has Many Names* (Philadelphia: Westminster, 1980), 27.
2. J. I. Packer, "What Do You Mean When You Say God?" *Christianity Today,* 19 September 1986, 3.

Bibliography

Agena, Kathleen. 1983. "The Return of Enchantment." *The New York Times Magazine*, 27 November; 66–80.

Babbie, Earl R. 1983. *Sociology: An Introduction*. Belmont, Calif.: Wadsworth.

Baer, Richard A., Jr. 1980. "TV: Carl Sagan's Narrow View of the Cosmos." *Wall Street Journal*, 24 October, 35.

Becker, Ernest. 1968. *The Structure of Evil: An Essay on the Unification of the Science of Man*. New York: George Braziller.

———. 1975. *Escape from Evil*. New York: Free Press.

Bellah, Robert N. 1967. "Civil Religion in America." *Daedalus* 96:1–21.

Berger, Peter L. 1963. *Invitation to Sociology*. New York: Doubleday.

———. 1967. *The Sacred Canopy*. New York: Doubleday.

———. 1969. *A Rumor of Angels*. Garden City, N.Y.: Doubleday.

———. 1974. *Pyramids of Sacrifice*. Garden City, N.Y.: Anchor, Doubleday.

———. 1978. "Ethics and the New Class." *Worldview* (April): 6–11.

———. 1980. *The Heretical Imperative*. Garden City, N.Y.: Anchor, Doubleday.

Benedict, Ruth. 1934. *Patterns of Culture*. Boston: Houghton-Mifflin.

Bonhoeffer, Dietrich. 1967. *Letters and Papers from Prison*. New York: Macmillan.

Bowen, Eleanor. 1954. *Return to Laughter*. New York: Harper.

Bronowski, Jacob. 1973. *The Ascent of Man*. Boston: Little, Brown.

Bruce-Briggs, B. 1979. *The New Class?* New Brunswick, N.J.: Transaction.

Burke, Peter. 1980. *Sociology and History*. Winchester, Mass.: Allen and Unwin.

Catton, William R. 1964. "The Development of Sociological Thought." In *Handbook of Modern Sociology*, edited by Robert E. L. Faris. New York: Rand McNalley.

Christianity Today. 1985. "Evangelical Leaders Judge Tony Campolo's Theology." 13 December, 52–54.

Colson, Charles. 1986. "Dear Pat: Winning isn't Everything." *Christianity Today*, 21 November 60.

Cousins, Norman. 1983. *The Healing Heart*. New York: Norton.

Cox, Harvey. 1965. *The Secular City*. New York: Macmillan.

———. 1977. *Turning East*. New York: Simon and Schuster.

DeSanto, Charles P., et al., eds., 1980. *A Reader in Sociology: Christian Perspectives*. Scottsdale, Pa.: Herald Press.

Dobson, Edward. 1986. "Christian Atheism." *Fundamentalist Journal* 5 (February): 12.

Dorn, Dean S. 1983. "The ASA code of Ethics and Textbooks in Sociology." *Teaching Newsletter* 8 (October): 6–8.

Durkheim, Emile. 1965. *Elementary Forms of the Religious Life.* New York: The Free Press.

Dyrness, William. 1983. *Christian Apologetics in a World Community.* Downers Grove: Ill.: Intervarsity Press.

Einstein, Albert. 1961. *Relativity: The Special and the General Theory.* New York: Crown Publishers.

Falwell, Jerry. 1980. *Listen America!* Garden City, N.Y.: Doubleday.

———. 1981. *The Fundamentalist Phenomenon.* Garden City, N.Y.: Doubleday.

———. 1983. *Old Fashioned Gospel Hour* Television program, 22 May.

Forell, George W. 1973. *The Proclamation of the Gospel in a Pluralistic World.* Philadelphia: Fortress Press.

Frankl, Victor. 1959. *Man's Search for Meaning: An Introduction to Logotherapy.* New York: Beacon Press.

———. 1967. *Psychotherapy and Existentialism.* New York: Washington Square Press.

Gellner, Ernst. 1985. *Relativism and the Social Sciences.* Cambridge: Cambridge University Press.

Geertz, Clifford. 1984. "Distinguished lecture: Anti Anti-Relativism." *American Anthropologist* 86 (June): 263–78.

Glover, David and Sheelagh Strawbridge. 1985. *The Sociology of Knowledge.* Ormstirk, Lancasthire: Causeway Press.

Goodenough, Ward H. 1970. *Description and Comparison in Cultural Anthropology.* Chicago: Aldine.

Gouldner, Alvin. 1978. "The New Class (Project 1 and 2)." *Theory and Society* (Fall).

Greeley, Andrew. 1972. *Unsecular Man: The Persistence of Religion.* New York: Schocken Books.

Griffin, Emilie. 1982. *Turning: Reflections on the Experience of Conversion.* Garden City, N.Y.: Doubleday.

Grunlan, Stephan A. 1982. "Biblical Authority and Cultural Relativity." In *Christian Perspectives on Sociology,* edited by Stephen A. Grunlan and Milton Reimer. Grand Rapids, Mich.: Zondervan Publishing House.

———. 1982. "Sociology and the Christian." In *Christian Perspectives on Sociology,* edited by Stephen A. Grunlan and Milton Reimer. Grand Rapids, Mich.: Zondervan Publishing House.

Hall, Edward T. 1966. *The Hidden Dimension.* Garden City, N.Y.: Doubleday.

Hanson, F. Allen. 1975. *Meaning in Culture.* Boston: Routledge and Keegan Paul.

Hatch, Elvin. 1983. *Culture and Morality: The Relativity of Values in Anthropology.* New York: Columbia University Press.

Hedley, R. C., and T. C. Traweggia. 1977. "Urges Revision of Ethical Code to Include Teaching and Student Rights." *Footnotes* 5 (October): 2–4.

Henry, Carl F. H. 1976. *God, Revelation, and Authority, Vol. 1.* Waco, Texas: Word Books.

———. 1982. *God, Revelation, and Authority, Vol. 5.* Waco, Texas: Word Books.

Herskovitz, Melvin. 1972. *Cultural Relativism: Perspectives in Cultural Relativism.* New York: Random House.

Hess, J. Daniel. 1980. *From the Other Point of View.* Scottsdale, Pa.: Herald Press.

Hick, John. 1980. *God Has Many Names.* Philadelphia: Westminster.

Hillary, George A., Jr. 1968. *Communal Organizations: A Study of Local Societies.* Chicago: University of Chicago Press.

Hoffer, Eric. 1951. *The True Believer.* New York: Harper and Row.

Horowitz, Irving. 1979. "On the Expansion of New Theories and the Withering Away of Old Classes." *Society* 16: 55–62.

Humanist Manifestos I and II. 1973. Buffalo, N.Y.: Prometheus Books.

Hunter, David E. and Phillip Whitten. 1976. *Encyclopedia of Anthropology.* New York: Harper and Row.

Hunter, James Davison. 1983. *American Evangelicalism: Conservative Religion and the Quandary of Modernity.* New Brunswick, N.J.: Rutgers University Press.

Ions, Edmund S. 1977. *Against Behaviorism: A Critique of Behavioral Science.* Totowa, N.J.: Rowman and Littlefield.

Johnson, Benton, 1977. "Sociological Theory and Religious Truth." *Sociological Analysis* 19: 368–88.

Johnson, Paul. 1983. *Modern Times: The World from the Twenties to the Eighties.* New York: Harper and Row.

Johnstone, Ronald L. 1975. *Religion and Science in Interaction: The Sociology of Religion.* Englewood Cliffs, N.J.: Prentice-Hall.

Kantzer, Kenneth S. 1985. "A Man of Zeal and Contradiction." *Christianity Today,* (20 September), 36–38.

Kaufman, Gordon. 1960. *Relativism, Knowledge, and Faith.* Chicago: University of Chicago Press.

Kelley, Dean M. 1972. *Why Conservative Churches Are Growing.* New York: Harper and Row.

Kleiman, Dena. 1981. "Parents' Groups Purging Schools of Humanist Books and Classes." *New York Times,* 17 May, 1.

Knox, Ronald A. 1949. *On Englishing the Bible.* London: Burns and Oates.

Koyama, Kosuke. 1974. *Waterbuffalo Theology.* Maryknoll, N.Y.: Orbis Books.

Kraft, Charles H. 1979. *Christianity in Culture: A Study in Dynamic Biblical Theologizing in Cross-Cultural Perspective.* Maryknoll, N.Y.: Orbis Books.

Kuhn, Thomas. 1970. *The Structure of Scientific Revolutions.* Chicago: University of Chicago Press.

LaHaye, Tim. 1980. *The Battle for the Mind.* Old Tappan, N.J.: Fleming H. Revel.

Lee, Alfred McClung. 1978. *Sociology for Whom?* New York: Oxford University Press.

Liebman, Robert C., and Robert Wuthnow. 1983. *The New Christian Right: Mobilization and Legitimation.* New York: Aldine Publishing Co.

Lyman, Stanford. 1978. *The Seven Deadly Sins: Society and Evil.* New York: St. Martins Press.

Lyman, Stanford, and Arthur Vidich. 1985. *American Sociology.* New Haven: Yale University Press.

Lyon, David. 1983. *Sociology and the Human Image.* Downers Grove, Ill.: Intervarsity Press.

McGehee, Charles L. 1982. "Spiritual Values and Sociology: When we Have Debunked Everything, What Then?" *American Sociologist* 17 (February): 40–46.

Mackay-Smith, Ann. 1985. "Schools are Becoming the Battleground in the Fight against Secular Humanism." *Wall Street Journal* (6 August), 31.

Nash, Ronald H. 1981. *The Word of God and the Mind of Man.* Grand Rapids, Mich.: Zondervan.

The National Commission on Excellence in Education. 1983. *A Nation at Risk: The Imperative for Educational Reform.* United States Department of Education (April).

Nida, Eugene A. 1952. *God's Word in Man's Language.* New York: Harper and Brothers.

Nida, Eugene A., and William Reyburn. 1981. *Meaning across Cultures.* Maryknoll, N.Y.: Orbis Books.

Niebuhr, H. Richard. 1946. *The Meaning of Revelation.* New York: Macmillan Company.

Nottingham, Elizabeth K. 1971. *Religion: A Sociological View.* New York: Random House.

Packer, J. I. 1986. "Good Pagans and God's Kingdom." *Christianity Today,* (7 January), 22–25.

———. 1986. "What Do you Mean When you Say God?" *Christianity Today,* (19 September), 27–31.

Parsons, Paul F. 1986. "Reading, Writing, and a Way of Life." *Christianity Today,* (7 November), 35–41.

Peshkin, Alan. 1986. *God's Choice: The Total World of a Fundamentalist School.* Chicago: University of Chicago Press.

Pierard, J. I. 1984. "Focus on the New Right." *Christian Century,* 10 October, 1930.

Pollard, William Grosvenor. 1961. *Physicist and Christian: A Dialogue Between the Communities.* New York: Seabury.

Quinney, Richard. 1980. *Providence: The Reconstruction of Social and Moral Order.* New York: Longman.

Reimer, Milton K. 1982. "The Study of Sociology: An Introduction." *Christian Perspectives on Sociology,* edited by Stephen A. Grunlan and Milton Reimer. Grand Rapids, Mich.: Zondervan Publishing House.

Rhea, Buford. 1981. *The Future of the Sociological Classics.* London: George Allen and Unwin.

Roberts, Keith A. 1974. *Religion in Sociological Perspective.* Homewood, Ill.: Dorsey Press.

Robinson, John A. T. 1963. *Honest to God.* London: SCM Press.

Ross, Edward A. 1907. *Sin and Society: An Analysis of Latter-Day Iniquity.* Boston: Houghton, Mifflin and Co.

Rothenberg, Stuart, and Frank Newport. 1984. *The Evangelical Voter, Religion and Politics in America.* Washington, D.C.: The Institute for Government and Politics.

Russell, Bertrand. 1957. *Why I am not a Christian and Other Essays on Religion and Related Subjects.* New York: Random House.

Sagan, Carl. 1980. *Cosmos.* New York: Random House.

Schaeffer, Francis A. 1982. *A Christian Manifesto.* Rev. ed. Westchester, Ill.: Crossway.

Schlessinger, Arthur, Jr. 1983. "Pretension in the President's Pulpit." *Wall Street Journal,* 17 March, 3.

Shepherd, William C. 1980. "Cultural Relativism, Physical Anthropology and Religion." *Journal for the Scientific Study of Religion* 19 (June):159–72.

Sider, Ron. 1986. "A New Covenant of Respect, Integrity, and Biblical Faithfulness." *Evangelicals for Social Action Newsletter* 1 November, 1–4.

Smith, Joe Carson. 1979. "Contextualization or Christ?" *Christian Standard* 114:427.

Spenier, Graham B., and Catherine S. Stump. 1978. "The Use of Research in Applied Marriage and Family Textbooks." *Contemporary Sociology* 7:553–62.

Stall, Stephen W. 1984. "Sociology of Knowledge, Relativism and Theology." In *Religion and the Sociology of Knowledge,* edited by Barbara Hargrove. New York: The Edwin Mellon Press.

Swatos, William H., Jr. 1980. "Liturgy and Lebensform: the Personal God as a Social Being." *Perspective in Religious Studies* 7:38–49.

————. 1984. *Faith of the Fathers: Science, Religion, and Reform in the Development of Early American Sociology.* Bristol, Ind.: Wyndham Hall Press.

Thistleton, Anthony C. 1980. *The Two Horizons.* Grand Rapids, Mich.: William B. Eerdmans.

Trueblood, Elton. 1975. *The Common Ventures of Life.* Waco, Texas: Word Books.

Webber, Robert E. 1982. *Secular Humanism: Threat and Challenge.* Grand Rapids, Mich.: Zondervan.

Weber, Max. 1949. *The Methodology of the Social Sciences.* New York: Free Press.

Zwier, Robert. 1982. *Born-Again Politics: The New Christian Right in America.* Downers Grove, Ill.: Intervarsity Press.

Index

Abraham: call of, 95; faith of, 87

Absolutes: and ethnocentrism, 50; existence of, 75–77; God's message as, 76

Absolutism: culturally transmitted, 133; danger of, 122; potential for, 132; as result of a vital culture, 133; as temptation, 140

Absolutists, Christian. *See* Christian absolutists

Absolutists, non-Christian, 22

Acts, book of, 112–15

Auschwitz, 19, 20

Australian aborigines, 50

Babbie, Earl R., 33

Baer, Richard, 34

Becker, Ernest, 32

Behavior: neither relative nor absolute, 122

Bellah, Robert, 139

Benedict, Ruth, 73

Berger, Peter: on chronocentrism, 90; on competing truth, 61; on epistemology, 63; on the failure of materialism, 152; on pluralism, 91; *Pyramids of Sacrifice,* 40; *The Sacred Canopy,* 24–25, 39; on sociology and debunking, 67; on sociology and relativity, 19–20

Bible, the: and cultural relativity, 85, 120, 126; and empirical knowledge, 144–45; and pluralism, 122–24, 155

Biblical interpretations by absolutists, 84–85

Biblical revelation: and Christian culture, 125–27; congruence of cultural relativity and, 86; cultural relativity as support for, 88

Biblical teaching: and acceptance of relativity, 122; and pluralism, 116–17

Biblical writers: reference to gods by, 122

Bonhoeffer, Dietrich, 24

Bowen, Eleanor, 16

Bronowski, Jacob, 20

Campolo, Tony, 123, 124

Christendom and Christian culture, 126

Christian absolutes and assertion of religion, 52

Christian absolutism: and biblical support, 83, 111, 114–15, 117–19; compromises biblical message, 125; danger of, 26; and fear of relativity, 133; importance of, 40; Jesus' teaching cited as support for, 108; and revelation, 88

Christian absolutists: background of students who are, 24; beliefs of, about relativists, 21; biblical interpretation used by, 84–85; commonality with community builders, 68; critique of cultural relativity by, 69–75; definition of beliefs of, 21–22; description of, 13–14; and justification for antagonism, 15; politics and, 25, 37; and revelation, 18; troubled by relativity, 123; variety of, 21–23; view of relativity, 19; view of the Bible, 85

Christian activism, 41

Christian fundamentalists: anthropological research conflict with, 51

Christianity: as a culture, 88, 134, 147; founded on events, 134; and the historical problem, 134; interest in countering chronocentrism, 149; religionless, 24; view of other religions, 155

Christian knowledge: scientific knowledge compared with, 29–30

Christians: liberal, 22; traditional-but-not-absolutist, 22

171

Christian schools: absolutist education in, 30

Christian truth and relativity, 52

Chronocentrism: as challenge to Christianity, 135; demystified by cultural relativity, 138; and ethnocentrism, 90–92; power of, 135; sociology's dangers of, 148–49

Circumcision, 116

Colson, Charles, 39

Comte, Auguste, 35

Conflict: polarizing effects of, 23; relativity does not resolve cross-cultural, 74–75

Context: importance of, 55

Conversation: and subjective reality, 64

Cornelius, 112

Cox, Harvey, 24, 41–42

Cultural anthropology: secular humanism and, 15

Cultural development: nonmechanical, 64

Cultural processes and the "people of God," 121

Cultural relativism: acceptance of, based on data, 58; as beneficial to Christians, 136–41; and Christian culture, 126; current status of, 57–59; effect of, 37; fear of, 84; preliminary definition of, 17; principle of, 16; produced by pluralism, 136; questioning absolutes, 19; relativity of, 58

Cultural relativists and fear of absolutism, 20–21

Cultural relativity: as absolute, 72–73; congruence of biblical revelation and, 86; consistent with the Bible, 120; and cross-cultural communication skills, 140; and demystification, 137; demystifies contemporary chronocentrism, 138; development of, 15–17, 49–55; empirical base for, 57; as an ethnocentric concept, 74; and failure to resolve cross-cultural conflict, 74–75; faith and the acceptance of, 89; identifies objective truth, 136; and knowledge, 18, 54; as method, 51; and the New Testament, 106–19; and objective moral standards, 51; and the Old Testament, 94–105; questions of the Bible and, 85; and relativity of individual conduct, 54; and reorientation of belief, 132; as self-contradictory, 73–74; and support for biblical revelation, 88; uncovers hidden assump-

tions, 92; view of revelation, 83–86

Culture: internalized, 88–90; the necessity of, 66

Dobson, Edward, 37

Durkheim, Emile, 24

Dyrness, William, 31

Einstein, Albert, 55, 132

Elijah, 101

Enculturation and knowledge, 54

Epistemology: importance of, 62–66

Ethical relativity: basis for, 69–72

Ethnocentrism: absolutes and, 50; and chronocentrism, 90–92; cultural relativity an example of, 74; development by anthropologists, 49–51; Jesus' challenge to, 111–12; Jesus' rejection of, 107; maintaining, 60; and missionary work, 61; and pastoral effectiveness, 61; social scientists attempt to avoid, 16

Evil spirits, 56

Faith: and the acceptance of cultural relativity, 89; and the food supply, 113

Falwell, Jerry, 25; on absolutes, 37–38; on fundamentalist growth, 40; on weaknesses of fundamentalists, 43

Food: cultural definition of, 65

Forell, George W., 62

Fox's Book of Martyrs, 70

Fundamentalism: growth of, 43–45

Fundamentalists: weaknesses of, 43

Fundamentals, The, 52

Geertz, Clifford, 57

Gideon, 101

Global village, 61; and pluralism, 136

Glover, David, 57, 138

God: biblical concept of, and cultural processes, 121; identity of, 97; as particular and universal, 95–96, 97

gods, foreign: Jacob and, 96; Jewish worship of, 99–100; Mosaic law and, 98

God's message as absolute, 76–77

Greeley, Andrew, 25, 40

Grunlan, Stephen A., 69–74, 83, 148

Habakkuk, 103

Hanson, F. Allen, 58, 59

Hare Krishna, 42

Hatch, Elvin, 57, 58, 73